D0742386

Play, Games, and Sport

THE LITERARY WORKS
OF LEWIS CARROLL

Two girls, like Alice, take seriously a favorite Victorian game. The illustration originally appeared in an anonymous, undated book, *Pictures for Our Pets: Home and Country Scenes*, published by the Religious Tract Society and illustrated by R. Barnes.

Play, Games, and Sport

THE LITERARY WORKS
OF LEWIS CARROLL

Kathleen Blake

CORNELL UNIVERSITY PRESS

Ithaca and London

Cornell University Press gratefully acknowledges
a grant from the Andrew J. Mellon Foundation
that aided in bringing this book to publication.

First published 1974 by Cornell University Press.
Published in the United Kingdom by Cornell University Press Ltd.,
2-4 Brook Street, London W1Y 1AA.

International Standard Book Number 0-8014-0834-2
Library of Congress Catalog Card Number 73-21362

Printed in the United States of America by York Composition Co., Inc.

Acknowledgments

I am grateful for permission to quote selections from the following: *A Selection from the Letters of Lewis Carroll (The Rev. Charles Lutwidge Dodgson) to His Child-Friends with Eight or Nine Wise Words about Letter-Writing*, edited with introduction and notes by Evelyn M. Hatch. © 1933. Used by permission of A. P. Watt & Son on behalf of the Lewis Carroll Estate.

The Annotated Alice by Lewis Carroll, edited by Martin Gardner. © 1960 by Martin Gardner. Used by permission of Crown Publishers, Inc.

The Humorous Verse of Lewis Carroll, The Rev. Charles Lutwidge Dodgson, New York: Dover Publications, 1960, an unabridged republication of *The Collected Verse of Lewis Carroll*. Copyright 1933 and renewed 1961 by Macmillan Publishing Co., Inc. Used by permission of Macmillan Publishing Co., Inc., and Macmillan Services, Ltd.

The Complete Works of Lewis Carroll, introduced by Alexander Woollcott, New York, 1937. Used by permission of Random House, Inc.

The Poetical Works of William Wordsworth, edited by Ernest de Selincourt, 2d edition, 1952. Used by permission of The Clarendon Press, Oxford.

The World of Mathematics, edited by James R. Newman. © 1956 by James R. Newman. Used by permission of Simon & Schuster, Inc.

5

KATHLEEN BLAKE

Seattle, Washington

Contents

Play, Games, and Sport

THE LITERARY WORKS
OF LEWIS CARROLL

Introduction

> Do you ever play at games? Or is your idea of life "breakfast, lessons, dinner, lessons, tea, lessons, bed, lessons, breakfast, lessons," and so on? It is a very neat plan of life and almost as interesting as being a sewing machine or a coffee grinder.

So Charles Dodgson wrote in a letter to May Forshall, one of his child-friends. He played at games himself: he carried an "in statuquo" board for chess on the train; he stocked his rooms at Tom Quad with musical boxes and mechanical toys, including a flying bat; according to Isa Bowman, another child-friend, backgammon was his passion. He was the originator of a whole string of games, published and unpublished: Court Circular, Croquet Castles (with affinities to Wonderland cards and croquet, by the way), Word-Links, Doublets, Lanrick, Syzygies, Blot-Backgammon, Thirdie Backgammon, a game played by moving letters about on a chessboard to form words, a game with the intriguing title Natural Selection. Photography was one of his hobbies, and he enjoyed photographing children at play. All this is interesting, though what Charles Dodgson did is less interesting than what Lewis Carroll wrote.

He wrote about games, and besides that much of his writing plays a game with the reader. *A Tangled Tale*, a hybrid of narrative and mathematics, is a quiz-game contest for its readers. The *Sylvie and Bruno* prefaces invite the reader to play a game with Carroll by guessing which segments were added as "padding" for the printer. The little manual *Eight or Nine Wise Words about Letter-Writing* is packaged in a trick envelope, a toy; one is invited to enjoy the "Pictorial Surprise" of beholding the Cheshire Cat disappear and the baby turn into a pig. Carroll published a symbolic logic textbook with a cardboard sheet and counters, for all the world like those of a board game. The poem "Jabberwocky" was very likely invented as part of a game of verse-making in the family parlor. And the *Alice* books are famously nondidactic and playful. Games abound in them, at various levels: there are the jokes and riddles, aimed as much at the reader as at Alice: "Jam tomorrow and jam yesterday—but never jam to-day"; "How is a raven like a writing desk?" The creatures share a mania for play, from the caucus-race on. Humpty-Dumpty treats conversation itself as a game. Cards, croquet, and chess establish the narrative frameworks of the novels.

Because play of all sorts infuses Carroll's imaginative literature, infuses meaning and structure and the author's attitude toward his work and his readers, I propose it as a theme worth tracking. This book asks, What did Carroll have in mind when he suggested to May Forshall that a great deal was missing, maybe everything, from a life of mechanical eating, work, and sleep, unless there was play? It asks the question in order, in the process of asking, to turn the answer(s) back on the literature. The point is to trace the literary shapes, taken one by one and taken together, cast by a playful aesthetic idea and a world view that sees games all around. And they were all around in nineteenth-century England, something I attempt to establish in order to provide a Victorian context for Carroll and his literary preoccupation with play, games, and sport.

Many studies of Wonderland and of its creator approach both with what Derek Hudson, in his book *Lewis Carroll*, rightly calls "prurient curiosity." I would like to have done with a version of Carroll which never lets us forget Dodgson's straitlaced and straight-as-a-poker ways and liking for female child-friends. This study does not really treat Dodgson at all, though from diaries, letters, and so on, shreds of the "real life" appear. It does treat Lewis Carroll, and I refer to him by the one name instead of the other. My purpose in doing so is not to enforce the schizophrenia theory: that Carroll was a sort of escapist alter ego, which implies there was a good deal to escape from in Dodgson. It is simply to give due precedence to the author over the man. By the same token, my approach is not psychoanalytical, though it can be termed psychological, since it considers Carroll's literary presentation of a psychic impulse, that of play.

The stranglehold on critical interest exercised by the personality of Rev. Charles Dodgson has been loosened in the last two decades, even though more biographical evidence is now available since the publication of the diaries in the fifties. Yet Carroll's minor works, lately widely bought in paperback, have received almost no interpretive attention as literature. They receive attention here. His most remarkable sustained poem, *The Hunting of the Snark*, has usually been allegorized in one way or another as a quest. Here it is considered as a hunt. The long, strange, last novels, the *Sylvie and Bruno* books, have drawn a mixture, scanty enough, of critical nods and bafflement. Here they are considered at some length—taken in their kaleidoscopically playful formal dimension and in relation to the theme of sport. The *Alice* novels have been often either taken two in one as a lump, or fragmented into bits to exercise philosophy on, or used as stimulus and excuse for essaying a style which hopes to be as "cute" as Carroll's. More recently, and more responsibly I think, they have been looked at for structures and themes compounding to form each narrative whole. Alice's growth process has come in for a variety of interpretations. The novels have been famously analyzed in Freudian terms. There are no phalluses, toilets, cannibals, wombs, or amniotic fluids, however, in the *Alices*; there are games. Elizabeth Sewell has made a start in doing justice to the importance of these games, and I owe to her *The Field of Nonsense* the recognition of just how important they are in the novels. But her study is an analysis of the genre of nonsense. My central chapters on how games shape the *Alices* in form and meaning are interpretations of the *Alices*, as the *Alices*, for themselves.

Carroll's writings reveal his awareness that, depending on one's motives, almost anything can be play—insofar as it is undertaken voluntarily, disinterestedly, for its own sake. He says, for example, in one of his essays, "I believe that any branch of science, when taken up by one who has a natural turn for it, will soon become as fascinating as sport to the ardent sportsman." His books of geometry and logic show that he has no first principles of reality to assert, because of what he calls the relativity of "axiomaticity." By the same token he presents logic not as a series of facts but as a series of agreements for the reader to enter into. Once agreed on terms and rules and limits, we have a sort of self-standing system which exists by fiat and can coexist with any number of possible other and even contradictory systems. We have in fact what Carroll called in his text of that name *The Game of Logic*.

At the outset of *Eight or Nine Wise Words* Carroll says Hoyle's golden rule for whist is the golden rule to be applied to real life: "When in doubt, win the trick." Carroll's advice is, when in doubt, make up one's letter register, an elaborately useless pastime that he proceeds to teach us. The attitude toward language reflected in this little piece seems to be that communication is a game system which is very difficult to master, and that what is needed is for both letter-writing parties to accept a set of stable rules. Once these are mastered, communication may become a game in which one can "win the trick" and triumph over someone else, as in the various ciphers that Carroll concocted for his child-friends. These were designed not for usefulness certainly but with a potential for delight or torture, depending which side one was on. Carroll wrote to one little girl, "Don't let Edith torture you with that funny way of writing, but tell her I'm going to send her a better way that'll make her hair stand on end with delight."

With an attitude like this about reality, about science, mathematics, logic, language, what wonder that Carroll writes Alice into a world that is a giant chessboard in *Through the Looking-Glass*? What wonder that her purpose in life is to advance from Pawn to Queen and to win the game? What wonder the riddles, conundrums, word-play? Considering the pervasiveness of play *in* Carroll's writing and the playing-a-game-with-the-reader attitude *of* much of it, I feel that a study must be promising which approaches his literature by way of the card game, the croquet match, the chessboard, the hunt.

Carroll's concept of play is the opposite of the view that can be conveniently isolated in the bestseller by Eric Berne, *Games People Play*. As Berne has it, "Pastimes and games are the substitutes for the real living of real intimacy." This attribution of fakeness to games because they are games is something we have to drop if we want to understand Carroll's fiction and if we want to avoid judging it, as Sewell, for example, sometimes falls into doing when she criticizes Carroll for never advancing beyond playing, and playing with everything.

Johan Huizinga's *Homo Ludens* offers a corrective to such a view. It insists on the serious nature of play and says that just because we know an activity to be play as we are playing does not render it a sham and us hypocrites. For example, Huizinga is at pains to show the playful nature of ritual, and he asserts that in a tribal ritual there exists the double knowledge that what is being enacted is not "real" and that it is not "not-real." Make-believe is not the same as delusion.

A realm without games, according to the broad thesis of *Homo Ludens*, would be a world without culture. Civilization is games. If Huizinga's thesis sounds too massive, take it another way. A game is a regularized social form engaged in, not out of necessity, but for pleasure—the elaboration of the superfluous. If we stop playing one set of games, don't we generally enter into some new arrangement, with some new set of terms, rules, and limits? If I do this, you may do this, that, or that. If you don't respond within some mutually understood and agreed-upon context, you are a spoilsport. You go right out of communication with me, that is, unless I agree to go over to your context and play that game. There is always the right of invention, one of the main lessons Alice learns. To Huizinga, to the linguist Ferdinand de Saussure, and, as I have suggested, to Carroll too, language itself is a gamelike system of reciprocally accepted terms and rules, arbitrary, meaningful only by social agreement. From this point of view a realm without games is hard to imagine. (Even work is generally surrounded and invaded by games.) Such a world can only be imagined as private. Applying *Homo Ludens* (and also Jaques Ehrmann's "*Homo Ludens* Revisited") to the purpose of understanding Carroll, we may conclude the inappropriateness of the dichotomy play/reality, and the inappropriateness of the common mental habit of attaching the idea "mere" to the words "play" and "games." Such an attachment is really very "Victorian," and here I use the word in a sense also common and inappropriate, as I will argue that Carroll was certainly a Victorian and yet advances almost no feeling of the mereness of play and games.

Huizinga's concept of man as *Homo ludens* comes from Schiller's seminal formulation in the *Aesthetic Letters*, where art is identified with play and even more broadly, "to declare it once and for all, Man plays only when he is in the full sense of the word a man, and *he is only wholly Man when he is playing.*" Schiller's Romantic theory received a recasting in the Victorian period by Herbert Spencer. Carroll read Spencer, although we can only guess whether he read that the aesthetic is specifically playful, that play can infuse all areas of activity, depending on the attitude of consciousness, that "no matter what the game, the satisfaction is in achieving victory—in getting the better of an antagonist. This love of conquest, so dominant in all creatures because it is the correlative of success in the struggle for existence, gets gratification from a victory at chess in the absence of ruder victories. . . . [Play] is carried on partly for the sake of the pleasure of the activity itself, and partly for the accompanying satisfaction of certain egoistic feelings which find for the moment no other sphere."

We know a great deal about the gospel of work bequeathed the Victorians by Carlyle (and by Utilitarianism, Evangelicalism, and Prince Albert), but Carlyle himself believed in Schiller's play spirit for a good while, also approving and emulating Jean-Paul Richter's skittish style. Charles Lamb wrote according to a playful aesthetic to be identified later by Walter Pater with art for art's sake, and John Ruskin praised "play—beautiful play—." Consider that the Victorians enjoyed the product of a much-expanded toy-and-game industry, that backgammon and charades flourished in the parlor, archery and croquet in the garden, football and cricket in the public schools and universities, field sports in the country. The "Morality of Muscularity" was vigorously preached along Darwinian/Spencerian lines, and a "Gospel of Amusement" was one of the enthusiasms of the day. (I am borrowing the delightful titles to two articles of the period, though one happens to be American.) In order to provide a context for Carroll, I have written a chapter on how Victorians played and how they thought of it, for the Victorian frame of mind was by no means all work and no play, even though many of us have fallen into the habit of attaching "earnest" to "Victorian" as if the one were the other's given name. Within this new context Carroll no longer appears as the anomaly he has sometimes been made out to be, but the chapter really offers only a beginning to the kind of research that needs to be done to reconstitute the lines of a gospel which approaches in importance the famous one on work.

The chapter on play, Victorianism, and Carroll comes last.

My principle of organization up to that conclusion includes method, model-making, and thesis. In the title of this book the three words really ought to be printed with arrows as connectives, left to right. The flow from play to sport is represented too in the progression of the chapters: Chapter 1, Play; Chapter 2, Games; Chapters 3–5, the *Alices* interpreted in the light of play and games; Chapter 6, Sport. The organization is developmental, although not biographically or artistically so. The progression follows that of the play impulse. In assuming a psychic chronology of play, I draw especially on Jean Piaget's *Play, Dreams and Imitation in Childhood*. The play impulse underlies games and sport, which are its further and later manifestations.

My psychological model of the play impulse is eclectically constructed; I use Freud, Groos, Erikson, Piaget, Huizinga, Ehrmann, Callois, Von Neumann, as well as Schiller and Spencer. My aim is not so much to convince the reader that this model makes sense (though I think it does) as to convince him that it makes sense, perhaps a new kind of sense, of what Carroll wrote. The model can be dryly epitomized as follows: play —spontaneous, disinterested, nonutilitarian—is characterized by a fundamental urge to mastery through incorporation of experience to the ego rather than by adjustment or accommodation of the ego to experience. Less dryly, if more roughly, the difference is between eating up life—for the pleasure, not the hunger—and being digested by it.

Since the model I am using is one of incorporation, defined first in the physical terms of eating, I begin the first chapter with Carroll's "Feeding the Mind" and proceed to analyze the evaluative distinction he makes between physical and mental incorporation, the one implying utility, mere mechanism, the other play, something more human and interesting.

If the first chapter or the first pages of the first chapter seem rather hard work and hard to swallow (especially for an introduction to play/eating), I can only say that this may be the nature of beginnings which lay ground and build models. The difficulty comes with the method, but after all one has to start with terms and rules.

The model established—urge to mastery through incorporation—the next question introduces the next stage of play and the second chapter. Would not an urge to mastery tend with the utmost naturalness to find expression in mastery of others? Some might answer no, but I think Carroll would be with Spencer in answering yes—the getting-the-better-of-an-antagonist theory. (Carroll once said *Alice* was about malice, and we know from his letters that his playfulness had in it an element of browbeating capable on occasion of reducing children to tears.) At the point where it takes two to play and one will win, we have a game. The chapters on the *Alices* follow the one on games, for these novels create a world of games, but of games going wild, edging into something else, where for instance the Queen of Hearts is so likely to win it's hardly worth Alice's while to play. This introduces the third stage of play and the sixth chapter. At the point where the game becomes so unbalanced that the one is playing, the other properly speaking being played, and the winner a foregone conclusion, we have sport, in Carroll's usual sense of the word, meaning cat-and-mouse, the hunt.

Model is method and both are thesis. Let me suggest somewhat further the direction in which we may expect these to take us. Carroll stands by the pervasiveness and humanity of play, and writes games into his literary worlds in proportion to their importance in his own world. The journals from mid-century tell us that they were increasingly important in Victorian England. If we didn't know it already from Carroll, *Blackwood's* will tell us: "A great revolution has been made. . . . Go where one will, whole families and their visitors are seen mallet in hand, whose great object in life, from the little girl of six to the grandpapa of sixty, seems to be to get through their hoops." The journals disputed the meaning and value of the amusement revolution. Carroll lines up with the game-playing faction. However, another faction received much attention in the press in the latter part of the century. This was the sport faction, and Carroll lines up in opposition to that.

Carroll endorses the innocence of play and games, by implication throughout his writing and straight out in one passage in *Sylvie and Bruno*. And yet their innocence is a problem for him, if after all they are related to sport. Quite the reverse of wanting a realm unconstrained in the rules of the social game, Carroll wishes that human activity could be better formalized and bound in by game constraints. (Such constraints are badly needed in Alice's dream worlds.) Stable terms, rules, and limits are needed because of the aggressiveness I think is implied by Carroll's idea of what's fun about playing in the first place. Whether he was himself as sweet and wholesome as he declared his relations with his child-friends to be (in my opinion both things are often questioned to no good end), we needn't think he was naive or utterly sentimental or hadn't read Spencer or heard of the survival of the fittest. An urge to mastery can't be trusted to generate only sweetness and wholesomeness. Pleasure can be had, without disaster, from the egoism and aggressiveness exercised for their own sakes which are the constituents of play psychology as long as social agreements to mutual restraint and observance of mutually accepted terms and rules obtain. But in the world of Carroll's imagination the fear is that if a state of "real living of real intimacy" (I am using Berne again) were to be arrived at, this would amount to a state too close to the intimacy of "off with their heads." The tendency of games by the very nature of their motive drive is to become sport, a version of play that Carroll does not hold innocent.

Another thing that isn't innocent is the masquerading of play—with its admittedly amoral though, Carroll hopes, containable impulses—as work. Not that to act out of playfulness is wrong. It may be the human thing to do. But to act, as Carroll says many scienists do, for example, as if proceeding out of altruistic duty, is to put others off their guard. Carroll wants to expose many activities as play in some form, not because he thinks they could or should be something else, but so that we might recognize when the games are not square, as Alice does, realize that they are manmade and can be changed, to the end that we learn to hold the line at games and avoid becoming, in our trust, the victims of a sporting instinct.

1. Play

"Feeding the Mind" and the
Joy of Being a Cause

In September 1884, Lewis Carroll delivered a lecture in the vicarage of Alfreton in Derbyshire. It was called "Feeding the Mind," its object to articulate the analogy between feeding the body with food and the mind with ideas. He treats the obvious points: the mind requires regular feeding and cannot continue healthy on a diet of mental sugarplums; mental gluttony, as well as starvation, is to be avoided; we should not mix up too many dishes at once; food is to be taken in at proper intervals and thoroughly chewed to prevent mental indigestion. There are some good bits: "I wonder if there is such a thing in nature as a FAT MIND? I really think I have met with one or two: minds which could not keep up with the slowest trot in conversation; could not jump over a logical fence to save their lives; always got stuck fast in a narrow argument; and, in short, were fit for nothing but to waddle helplessly through the world" (FM, p. 21).[1] From this quotation it can be inferred that a well-fed mind would be one that could keep up—not so much with the practicalities of life as with its social recreations: its conversational races, its logical hurdles, its argumentative competitions. In short, to be "fit" is not to be "helpless," not to lose out.

[1] "Feeding the Mind," with pref. note by William H. Draper (London, 1907); hereafter identified in the text as FM, with page reference.

The most obvious and most significant point for my purposes in "Feeding the Mind" is that, all qualifications and regulations and warnings aside, Carroll advocates eating. Why? What's good about eating is that something chewed, swallowed, digested is *yours*. Assimilation equals gratification, all the more so if you do it when you don't have to by nature. In spite of a utilitarian ring to notions like feeding the mind in the interest of health, Carroll's lecture is not really concerned with usefulness in the ordinary sense. It is concerned with pleasure. When you feed the mind as you might the body, for the fun of the feeding, you are moving toward play.

The little treatise on feeding the mind is an interesting place to begin in view of the preoccupation with food noticed by most commenters on Carroll and his works. This preoccupation is a favorite in psychological criticism. Besides the split personality, archetypal quest, birth trauma, oedipal, phallic, and anal interpretations, there is also an interpretation that concentrates on the oral theme in the *Alices*, particularly on the aspect of oral aggressiveness. For example, Phyllis Greenacre in *Swift and Carroll* stresses under the heading "Attitudes toward Eating and Breathing" what she views as the sinister fixation upon these forms of incorporation expressed in Carroll's life and works. She cites a letter from Carroll to Gertrude Chataway in which he works around to a quite vampirishly literal interpretation of the phrase "I will drink your health." Later Greenacre remarks the "primitive oral cannibalistic aggression . . . obvious in the *Alice* books."[2]

[2] Greenacre, *Swift and Carroll* (New York, 1955), pp. 172–181, 254; her citation of the letter to Gertrude Chataway, p. 176, is from Stuart Dodgson Collingwood, *The Life and Letters of Lewis Carroll (Rev. C. L. Dodgson)*, illus. (New York, 1899), p. 301. See also Virginia Woolf, "Lewis Carroll," in *The Moment and Other Essays* (New York, 1948), pp. 81–84; Sidney Halpern, "The Mother-Killer," *Psychoanalytic Review*, LII (Summer 1965), 71–74; Ernest Earnest, "The Walrus and the Carpenter," *CEA Critic*, XXVI (Dec. 1963), 1, 6–7, and Judith Bloomingdale,

Such a view was first presented in full psychoanalytic dress by Paul Schilder in his "Psychoanalytic Remarks on *Alice in Wonderland* and Lewis Carroll." Schilder believes that *Wonderland* is a book full of anxiety. Alice is continually frustrated: "It is perhaps remarkable that she is never successful when she wants to eat." On the other hand, "Oral aggressiveness is found everywhere." Some examples include: the Walrus and the Carpenter eating the oysters, Alice mentioning a mouse-eating cat to the Mouse, the owl being devoured by the panther, little fish by the crocodile. Schilder concludes from his brief survey of these "preponderant oral sadistic trends of cannibalistic character" that the book is perhaps too reinforcing of destructiveness to be safe for children.[3]

Regarding this conclusion, I am with Joseph Wood Krutch, who questions Schilder's solemn warning. *Alice* has more than once been characterized as a book terrifying to children. Katherine Anne Porter is a notable spokesman for this point of view. But Krutch says he has never heard of a child dangerously terrified by *Alice*, and he feels that far from inculcating destructiveness, the book merely demonstrates that a child is never too young to laugh at those morbid fears which psychoanalysts tell us he is never too young to fear.[4]

"Alice as *Anima*: The Image of Woman in Carroll's Classics," in *Aspects of Alice: Lewis Carroll's Dreamchild as Seen through the Critics' Looking-Glasses, 1865–1971*, ed. Robert Phillips (New York, 1971), pp. 378–390; John Skinner, "Lewis Carroll's Adventures in Wonderland," *American Imago*, IV (Dec. 1947), 3–31; Martin Grotjahn, "About the Symbolization of Alice's Adventures in Wonderland," *American Imago*, IV (Dec. 1947), 32–41; and Albert Cook, *The Dark Voyage and the Golden Mean: A Philosophy of Comedy* (New York, 1966), p. 128; Kenneth Burke, "The Thinking of the Body: Comments on the Imagery of Catharsis in Literature," *Psychoanalytic Review*, L (Fall 1963), 375–418.

[3] Schilder, "Psychoanalytic Remarks on *Alice in Wonderland* and Lewis Carroll," *Journal of Nervous and Mental Disease*, LXXXVII (Feb. 1938), 161–162.

[4] Krutch, "Psychoanalyzing Alice," *The Nation*, CXLIV (Jan. 30, 1937),

In itself the oral theme in Carroll's works does not call out for reexamination. It is well known that Alice is a little girl "who always took a great interest in questions of eating and drinking."[5] Still, bearing with us such grains of salt as those provided by Krutch, we can learn something about Carroll's fiction by looking at the psychology of eating, at least insofar as it helps illuminate the psychology of play.

Let me pave the way in theory. According to Freud's "Instincts and Their Vicissitudes" the first stage of infant development is "the phase of incorporation or devouring, a type of love which is compatible with abolishing the object's separate existence and which may therefore be described as ambivalent," that is, expressive of both libido and aggressivity. It seems to me that Freud often hints at the existence of an instinct even more integral and primary than these two—the two represented in his final bipolar instinctual theory as eros and death. Once for example in *Civilization and Its Discontents*, Freud explains aggressivity as the expression of an instinct yet more fundamental, which he calls the ego's "old wishes for omnipotence." Again, in "Beyond the Pleasure Principle" he refers to "the instinct for mastery."[6]

129–130; see also his "Lewis Carroll's Subconscious," review of Roger Lancelyn Green's ed. of *The Diaries of Lewis Carroll*, *The Nation*, CLXXVIII (March 27, 1954), 262–263; Katherine Anne Porter, Bertrand Russell, Mark Van Doren, "Lewis Carroll, *Alice in Wonderland*," in *The New Invitation to Learning*, ed. Mark Van Doren (New York, 1942), p. 208.

[5] Carroll, *Alice's Adventures in Wonderland*, in *The Annotated Alice*, illus. John Tenniel, introd. and notes Martin Gardner (New York, 1960), p. 100.

[6] Sigmund Freud, "Instincts and Their Vicissitudes," *The Standard Edition of the Complete Psychological Works of Sigmund Freud*, trans. under general editorship of James Strachey, in collaboration with Anna Freud, assisted by Alex Strachey and Alan Tyson, 24 vols. (London, 1957), XIV, 138; *Civilization and Its Discontents*, *Works*, XXI, 121; "Beyond the Pleasure Principle," *Works*, XVIII, 16.

That this instinct is the basis for love as well as for aggressiveness is suggested in the passage quoted from "Instincts and Their Vicissitudes." After his discussion of love's ambivalent oral stage, Freud goes on to say, "At the higher stage of pregenital sadistic-anal organization, the striving for the object appears in the form of an *urge for mastery*, to which injury or annihilation of the object is a matter of indifference. Love in this form and at this preliminary stage is hardly to be distinguished from hate in its attitude towards the object" (italics mine).[7]

This description of the double operation of the urge for mastery applies very well to the oral approach, in which attraction, or love, expresses itself by way of introjection. The result of this incorporation, however, is identical with the result of the opposite response of repulsion, which involves the removal of the object (whether by removal of oneself or it). Introjection, however loving, means annihilation of the object. "Mourning and Melancholia" gives us this paradox: "The ego wants to incorporate this object into itself, and in accordance with the oral or cannibalistic phase of libidinal development in which it is, it wants to do so by devouring it."[8]

Building on Freud, Erik Erikson says of the first stage of life: "To him [the baby] the oral zone . . . is only the focus of a first and general mode of approach, namely, incorporation." The mode of approach Erikson here formulates reflects a primary impulse toward mastery, which antedates either love or aggressiveness, and of which both are expressions. According to Erikson perhaps the most fundamental need is "the ego's need to master the various areas of life." Eating asserts such mastery, since it makes the object serve the physical needs of the organism. Erikson demonstrates too how this need for mastery is extended from the physical to the mental/emotional sphere. Specifically, Erikson identifies play as the purest

[7] Freud, *Works*, XIV, 138–139.
[8] Freud, *Works*, XIV, 249–250.

extension of the incorporative mode of approach. "To hallucinate ego mastery and yet also to practice it in an intermediate reality between phantasy and actuality is the purpose of play." Play expresses Freud's "urge for mastery" in a purer form even than work since the latter is still related to satisfaction of physical need, like eating, whereas play is the assertion of mastery for its own sake.[9]

Erikson gives Freud's instance of a boy at play who acts out mastery of a situation in which, actually, he is a passive sufferer. The boy, frustrated because his mother is leaving him ("*fortsein*"), plays at "*fortsein*" with all his toys. Since he makes them go away, he also presumably enjoys the power to make them come back again. He converts his role from passive to active and replaces his former impotent frustration with a pleasing sense of control. The incident shows that while play belongs to the pleasure rather than the reality principle, it by no means always involves the acting out of pleasant experiences; its first purpose is to master what is uncontrolled by the ego. Freud says in "Beyond the Pleasure Principle," "It is clear that in their play children . . . , as one might put it, make themselves master of the situation."[10]

Pleasing here is what Karl Groos aptly phrases in *The Play of Man*: "the joy of being a cause." Groos also says that even the simplest kind of play—"hustling things about"—is instinctually gratifying: "The primitive impulse to extend the sphere of their power as far as possible leads men to the conquest and control of objects lying about them." By the same token, catching and throwing rouse feelings of "our supremacy over matter."[11]

Jean Piaget's theory of play, like Erikson's, makes explicit the analogy between incorporation, or assimilation (as of

[9] Erikson, *Childhood and Society*, 2d ed., rev. and enlarged (New York, 1963), pp. 72, 211, 212.

[10] Freud, *Works*, XVIII, 14–17.

[11] Groos, *The Play of Man* (New York, London, 1914), pp. 152, 95, 118.

food), and play. In *Play, Dreams and Jmitation in Childhood* Piaget defines play as the pole of behavior characterized by assimilation; the contrasting pole is accommodation to reality. (A sort of rough gloss on the meanings of assimilation and accommodation is offered by the old Earl of *Sylvie and Bruno:* " 'A child's first view of life . . . is that it is a period to be spent in accumulating portable property. That view gets modified as the years glide away.' ") Progressively more sophisticated types of mental incorporation are understood in terms of the simple physical model of eating. There are three stages of play. In discussing the earliest-appearing type—sensory/motor practice play (hustling things about)—Piaget says, "There was merely assimilation to the activity itself, *i.e.*, use of the phenomenon for the pleasure of the activity, and that is play." The function of the second type—symbolic play (imitation, fantasy)—is also "to assimilate reality to the ego while freeing the ego from the demands of accommodation." Although for Piaget the third stage—games with rules (regular social games)—represents a decline of children's play, since it implies relative weakening of egocentric control because of the compulsion of the rules and the constraints imposed by reciprocity, still such games are a form of play, and "the function of play is to protect this universe [that of playful assimilation of reality to the ego] against forced accommodation to ordinary reality." Piaget's play world is one of mastery, the kind of mastery that can be understood when one thinks in the nontechnical terms of eating up experience, rather than being digested by it.[12]

[12] Piaget, *Play, Dreams and Jmitation in Childhood*, trans. G. Gattegno and F. M. Hodgson (New York, 1962), pp. 89, 92, 134, 168; Carroll, *Sylvie and Bruno*, illus. Harry Furniss (London, 1890). Others besides Erikson and Piaget develop the relationship between physical and mental incorporation. For example, a similar idea has been presented in popularized, oversimplified form in Eric Berne's *Games People Play: The Psychology of Human Relationships* (New York, 1964). Robert Wälder ("The

Carroll shows children at play in its more primitive, unstructured sense in his photographs: Agnes Price and Florence Bainbridge with their dolls, Alice and Lorina Liddell on a teeter-totter, and Cyril Bickersteth on his wooden horse. Another, called "Tired of Play," shows Mary and Constance Ellison asleep beside their ball and bat. (Carroll's rooms at Tom Quad contained many toys, puzzles, and novel devices for children to play with. Carroll was well stocked with clockwork automata and musical boxes, popular and ever more available at this time. One of the most celebrated was a flying mechanical bat which one day flew out of his window to alight on a tea tray being carried across the square below. At least one toy is memorialized in an individual photographic study, " 'Tim' the Family Doll.") [13]

Paging through Helmut Gernsheim's album of selections, *Lewis Carroll, Photographer*, we see photograph after photograph of children playacting scenes, à la the symbolic play of Piaget. Alice Jane Donkin, emerging caped from an upper-story window, balanced lightly by the fingers of one hand

---

Psychoanalytic Theory of Play," *Psychoanalytic Quarterly*, II [1933], 208–224) supports the idea of egoistic pleasure through exercise of the instinct of mastery in play and employs an eating model for this type of incorporation. He stresses play's nonaccommodation to reality and its amorality. See also Allen Sapora and Elmer Mitchell, *Theory of Play and Recreation*, 3d ed. (New York, 1961), pp. 91, 104–105. This more recent work states that play constitutes activity in which man has a feeling of mastery and reasonable assurance of success. This is part of Mitchell's and Mason's self-expression theory but resembles other theories summarized in the book, for example, Franz Alexander's psychoanalytic theory, which is partially based on Erikson's clinical observations. According to Alexander, play is a manifestation of activity not needed for survival, productive of functional gratification in mastery of unsolved situations.

[13] Helmut Gernsheim, *Lewis Carroll, Photographer*, illus. (New York, 1949), plates 34, 55 (Price, Bickersteth); Stuart Dodgson Collingwood, ed., *Diversions and Digressions of Lewis Carroll* (formerly titled *The Lewis Carroll Picture Book*), illus. (New York, 1961), plates 6, 7, 10, 14 ("Tim," Bainbridge, Ellison, Liddell).

upon the window frame, and one foot reaching for the top rung of a dangling rope ladder, poses for "The Elopement." It looks quite dangerous, because the scene is being played with every sort of realism. Other pictures show Agnes Weld portraying Little Red Riding Hood, Wicliffe Taylor as a sort of helmeted baby knight with a spear, and Xie Kitchen as a Chinaman. One of Carroll's most elaborate composite scenes pictures the children of the Reverend Kitchen in a tableau vivant (favorite get-up of Victorian parties and pleasure-makings) of St. George on his rocking horse slaying the dragon and rescuing the damsel. Carroll maintained a wardrobe of costumes for dressing up his small subjects. Because the wet-plate collodion process that he used was cumbersome, he would have had difficulty photographing children at unstaged play, so that he was limited for the most part to the effects obtainable from lengthily held poses in his rooms at Tom Quad. He therefore created simulations or set-pieces, which no doubt profited from the reality of the children's pleasure in such fantasy.[14]

Carroll's diaries also attest to his interest in stageplay. He traveled often by train to London for the shows at the Princess, the Haymarket, Drury Lane. He liked children's theater and child actors, and he may have refused full holy orders partly because they must be assumed at the expense of his playgoing.[15] Certainly there is evidence of Carroll's fascination with play broadly defined, though it is not symbolic or mimetic play but games with rules that figure most in his writing. No matter what the type of play, Piaget's basic assimilative model is well suited to explain Carroll's playful approach to things.

Piaget illustrates the contrasting modes, accommodation and assimilation, by saying that accommodation, which means

[14] Gernsheim, plates 15, 10, 18, 62; Collingwood, ed., *Diversions and Digressions*, plate 34.

[15] Derek Hudson, *Lewis Carroll* (London, 1954), pp. 116–118.

essentially adjustment to the reality "out there," finds characteristic expression in scientific empiricism and induction but that mathematics and logic exemplify assimilation since they entail deduction, incorporation of phenomena into preconstructed mental schemes. They offer the purer instance of mental digestion of reality to a form organized around and validating an unchanged digester. Lewis Carroll, as Charles Lutwidge Dodgson, was after all a mathematician and a logician.[16]

Although "Feeding the Mind" does not mention play or games as such, Carroll here, as almost everywhere else, presents mental activity as a form of incorporation rather than accommodation. I am not thinking only of the obvious analogy between the incorporative process of eating and that of its mental equivalent. Perhaps even more revealing is the fact that the treatise does not present mental feeding as a means of dealing with or adjusting to reality; its final test is not that it is useful. Rather, Carroll's test case of good mental feeding involves the following example: Take a man being quizzed on some fact, say English history; if he has not fed his mind properly, he will, in dipping into his memory, become "hopelessly twisted up and entangled." After several embarrassing false tries, he must be reduced to awkward silence and then to the stammering half-answers of desperation. He loses control. To Carroll's way of thinking he loses the encounter. "And all this for want of making up his knowledge into proper bundles and ticketing them," that is, for want of that tidy logical or mathematical schematization which Piaget associates with mental incorporation. One who had properly digested facts in his mind, according to Carroll, would have emerged triumphant—master of English history, not for the sake of its inherent interest or of its usefulness in helping him accommo-

[16] Piaget, p. 161. Alfred Binet draws the general analogy between the psychology of mathematicians and of chessplayers in *Psychologie des grands calculateurs et joueurs d'échecs* (Paris, 1894).

date to reality, but, it seems, for the sake of the mastery itself (FM, pp. 26–28).

At the beginning of "Feeding the Mind" Carroll draws a significant distinction: we are sure to feed the body because nature internalizes its demands to be fed, but the same is not true for the mind, for "we can continue to exist as animals (scarcely as men) though the mind be utterly starved and neglected." Carroll thus strongly implies that of the two forms of incorporation that which is mental and not aimed at mere physical self-preservation is what makes us human (FM, pp. 15–16).

Piaget does not discuss this evaluative difference between the forms of incorporation; he does not point out the utilitarian aspect of physical incorporation by way of contrast with mental incorporation, which is done for fun, not to live. This important distinction, however, does appear in Schiller's famous formulation in *On the Aesthetic Education of Man*: he contrasts activity performed out of need and that performed for its own sake. This contrast between work and play he finds already in germinal form in the animal world: "The animal *works* when deprivation is the mainspring of its activity, and it *plays* when the fullness of its strength is this mainspring, when superabundant life is its own stimulus to activity." Again, ornamental display and play are "evidence of an external freedom, for as long as necessity dictates and want impels, imagination is bound with strong chains to the actual," and ornament and play are "also evidence of an internal freedom, since they reveal to us a force which sets itself in motion of its own accord, independently of any outward material, and possesses sufficient energy to repel the pressure of matter." Schiller anticipates Freud's passivity→activity model: "a nature which delights in appearance and play no longer takes pleasure in what it receives, but in what it does." In sum, "to declare it once and for all, Man plays only when he is in the true sense of the word a man, and *he is only wholly Man*

when he is playing." Man is to be identified not solely as
Homo faber or *Homo sapiens,* but as *Homo ludens.* This
classification, which serves as the title for Johan Huizinga's important book, is founded on a view of the human significance of
play stemming largely from Schiller.[17]
Whether Carroll held such a view as a conscious theory is
questionable and not very important, as also whether he might
have read and derived it from Schiller. If influence is to be
looked for, it would more likely be found coming from Herbert
Spencer rather than from Schiller. That Carroll read Spencer
seems certain, though his diary does not tell us what and how
much. In *Sylvie and Bruno* (1889) he has fun with Spencer's
high-flown evolutionary philosophy by garbling it into a conversation between a pseudolearned lady, who is apparently
plagued with extremely weak mental digestion, and an exas-
perated young man, who is trying to put an end to her preten-
tions once and for all by confounding her with "Sillygisms"
from Spencer. But if Carroll laughed at Spencer, he did not
totally reject certain of his ideas, for instance those on evolution or on writing style.[18]

[17] Freidrich Schiller, *On the Aesthetic Education of Man in a Series of
Letters,* trans. with introd. Reginald Snell (New York, 1965), pp. 133,
125, 80; see Huizinga, "Foreward," *Homo Ludens: A Study of the Play-
Element in Culture* (Boston, 1950). Carl Jung agrees that creativity is
fundamentally play: "The creative activity of the imagination frees man
from his bondage to the 'nothing but' and liberates in him the spirit of
play. As Schiller says, man is completely human only when he is playing"
(*Modern Man in Search of a Soul,* trans. W. S. Dell and Cary F. Baynes
[New York, 1933], p. 76).
[18] Carroll, *Sylvie and Bruno,* pp. 258–259. Carroll was happy to have
evolutionary theory, particularly natural selection, reconciled with belief in
God. In his diary he notes, for example, his appreciation for Sir George
Mivart's *Genesis of the Species,* which he says performs such a reconciliation (Nov. 1, 1894, in *The Diaries of Lewis Carroll,* ed. and supplemented Roger Lancelyn Green, 2 vols. [New York, 1954], II, 334). Carroll's article "Some Popular Fallacies about Vivisection" (1875) shows
us that he does not wish to deny that "man is twin-brother to the mon-

Possibly Carroll was familiar with Spencer's "Aesthetic Sentiments," published in 1872 as part of *The Principles of Psychology*. Spencer opens this Victorian restatement of Schiller's *Aesthetic Letters* by announcing that he can't remember the name of "a German author" who planted the notion in his mind that "aesthetic sentiments originate from the play-impulse." He identifies play and aesthetic activities in that "neither subserve, in any direct way, the processes conducive to life." Even though, he says, ulterior benefits may accrue, these do not motivate the actions as such.[19]

---

key" but that he does want to logically corner the scientists responsible for this theory into at least being consistent and giving "the anthromorphized ape the benefit of the argument," by pronouncing animal and human suffering as the same in kind and therefore equally to be avoided. Carroll fears that the scientific attitude (whose possible closer relationship to play rather than to work motives will be discussed in Chapter 6) will eventually tempt men to use evolutionary theory to justify quite an opposite position: that is, if men are but animals, then man is as eligible a subject for vivisection as any beast. See *The Complete Works of Lewis Carroll*, illus. John Tenniel, introd. Alexander Woollcott (New York, 1937), p. 1192; this volume is far from complete, but since it is the most complete edition of Carroll, I will use it unless there is a particular reason, for instance the illustrations, for referring to a separate edition of one of his works. For further evidence that Carroll accepted some of Spencer's ideas, we may look to "Feeding the Mind," where he suggests that a brief break or variation in concentration rests the mind enough to restore it to proper functioning. Spencer expresses a similar idea in "The Philosophy of Style," *Westminster Review* (Oct. 1852), rprt. in *Essays Scientific, Political and Speculative*, Library ed., 3 vols. (New York, 1901), II, 333–369. The idea is quite commonplace; still it is possible Carroll had read Spencer.

[19] Spencer, "Aesthetic Sentiments," *The Principles of Psychology*, 3d ed., 2 vols. (London, Edinburgh, 1890), II, 627–648. That by "a German author" Spencer means Schiller is corroborated by Benedetto Croce, *Aesthetic as Science of Expression and General Linguistics*, trans. Douglas Ainslie, rev. ed. (New York, 1960), p. 388. While this essay of Spencer's appeared after Carroll had written his most famous works, the ideas are essentially developments of ones which Carroll might have run into much

The *Alices* are famous for being playful and moral-less; they are without explicit ulterior motive or benefit. But although the books are nondidactic (relative to the heavy-handed moralism of most children's literature of the time), they do bear a relation to reality and say something about life. Even a parlor game has a meaning. In *"Homo Ludens* Revisited," Jaques Ehrmann makes the very good point that while games are not utilitarian in the practical sense, they have psychological utilities continuous with those in the real world. In fact, they are part of the real world, part of the same economy of values. Play is often defined as gratuitous, but this is only by contrast to work. Actually it is wrong to conceive of play as without consequences. The habit of thought which causes the word "mere," expressed or unexpressed, to hover about the word "play" should be broken.[20]

earlier. For example, "Use and Beauty," first published in *The Leader* (Jan. 2, 1852), rprt. in *Essays Scientific, Political* and *Speculative*, II, 370–374, offers in brief form the germ of Spencer's later-to-be-developed notion concerning the nonutilitarian nature of the aesthetic. For another clear statement of this view, see "The Purpose of Art," in the collection of published and unpublished writings in *Facts and Comments* (New York, 1902), pp. 44–49; here Spencer rejects Matthew Arnold, Holman Hunt, and those musicians who think that art should elevate, teach. Though it may produce transitory side effects of a beneficial kind, concludes Spencer, "the primary purpose of music [or other arts] is neither instruction nor culture but pleasure; and this is an all-sufficient purpose" (p. 48). Karl Groos thinks along lines similar to Spencer's: though he emphasizes throughout *The Play of Man* the biological and social uses of play—a kind of practice for the future—he is careful to reiterate that these uses do not provide the actual motives for playing.

[20] Ehrmann, *"Homo Ludens* Revisited," *Yale French Studies*, Game, Play, Literature issue, n. 41 (Summer 1968), 42–44. On Victorian children's literature see, for example, F. J. Harvey Darton, *Children's Books in England, Five Centuries of Social Life*, 2d ed. (Cambridge, 1966), pp. 54, 268; Roger Lancelyn Green, "The Golden Age of Children's Books," in *Essays and Studies Collected for the English Association by Beatrice White* (London, 1962), n.s. XV, 64; Amy Cruse, "A Young Vcitorian's Library," in *The Victorians and Their Reading* (Boston, 1935), p. 305; Muriel Kent,

However, it is not necessary to equate the *Alice* books with parlor games simply because they revolve about parlor games. *A Tangled Tale* represents a more total equivalence of literature and game. True, many times in the *Alices* Carroll is playing with the reader. For example, "Jabberwocky" could be considered a puzzle game for the reader as well as for Alice to figure out; the same goes for many of the conundrums and jokes. But if the *Alice* books are a game, they are a game that frustrates the reader, for what they are about is not experience as a game that operates as expected and desired, but rather one that doesn't.

The *Alices* and the *Snark* may mean, if not teach. Their meanings are imbedded in their structures rather than in direct messages. Although some of Carroll's books are meant to teach directly and seem to be useful in the ordinary sense, for example *Symbolic Logic* (1896), which aims to instruct children in the elements of the discipline, characteristically even here he offers logic first and foremost as "Mental recreation," a kind of superior game, better, he tells us, even than backgammon, chess, and halma. Its superiority lies in the ulterior benefits which may accrue—the convenience as a mental occupation always at hand, of absorbing interest, and of "use" to one in any subject taken up. This "use," though, is not one directed

"The Art of Nonsense," *Cornhill Magazine*, CXLIX (April, 1934), 478–487; Elsie Leach, "Alice in Wonderland in Perspective," *Victorian Newsletter*, XXV (Spring 1964), 9–11; Corneilia Meigs, Anne Thazter Eaton, Elizabeth Nesbitt, and Ruth Hill Viguers, *A Critical History of Children's Literature: A Survey of Children's Books in English*, decorations Vera Bock, rev. ed. (London, 1969), p. 194; of these the latter two give particularly strong statements of the contrast between Carroll's and the typical moralizing Victorian literature for children. See also Carroll's letter to Mary Brown, March 2, 1880, in *A Selection from the Letters of Lewis Carroll (The Rev. Charles Lutwidge Dodgson) to His Child-Friends with "Eight or Nine Wise Words about Letter-Writing,"* ed. with introd. and notes Evelyn M. Hatch (London, 1933), p. 165, and letters to Florence Balfour, to the Lowrie children, and to Mary Barber, pp. 98, 243–245.

at practical accommodation to reality. Rather, symbolic logic is useful mostly in enabling one to assert one's mental powers; it gives the clearness "to see your way through a puzzle," the habit of arranging your ideas in an "orderly and get-at-able form" (compare the mental bundling and ticketing in "Feeding the Mind"), and the power to detect fallacies in other people's arguments (hence preventing one's being imposed upon, and, in effect, allowing one to triumph over the less logical). All of these uses strike me as first psychological, and only practical as a quite incidental second—included in the preface to vindicate the book's seriousness. *Symbolic Logic* is simply an extended version of the original, which is revealingly titled *The Game of Logic* (1887). Carroll's logic books demonstrate the successful operation of games shown baffling and baffled in the *Alices*.[21]

As Spencer points out, playful or aesthetic activity is not essentially different from serious or utilitarian activity: "The same [mental] agencies are in action; and the only difference is in the attitude of consciousness." The following passage from Spencer's essay expresses what a game attitude is and how it can be extended over very large territories of experience; it says a lot about what goes on in Carroll's books:

> No matter what the game, the satisfaction is in achieving victory—in getting the better of an antagonist. This love of conquest, so dominant in all creatures because it is the correlative of success in the struggle for existence, gets gratification from a victory at chess in the absence of ruder victories. Nay we may even see that playful conversation is characterized by the same element. In banter, in repartee, in "chaff," the almost-constant trait is some display of relative superiority. Through a wit-combat

---

[21] Carroll, "Introduction to Learners," *Symbolic Logic Part J, Elementary* (London, 1896), p. xiii; cf. Carroll, *The Game of Logic* (London, New York, 1887).

there runs the effort to obtain mental supremacy. That is to say, this activity of the intellectual faculties in which they are not used for purposes of guidance in the business of life, is carried on partly for the sake of the pleasure of the activity itself, and partly for the accompanying satisfaction of certain egoistic feelings which find for the moment no other sphere.

As Carroll is perhaps hinting in a letter to Lucy Wilcox, a playful attitude may be introduced into many areas from which it is customarily excluded: "Why shouldn't we enjoy things we 'have to' do?" He is referring to an excursion which his friend forced him into taking and which turned out to be a "sandwich" of pleasure in his monotonous life. With a switch in mental stance we may transform what was obligation and duty into play.[22]

Another of Spencer's points can be directly related to "Feeding the Mind." Spencer discusses the sense impressions and their relative aesthetic (playful) capabilities. Interestingly, he observes that we seldom call a taste beautiful. (It is conceivable but barely, as in the beautiful soup of the Mock Turtle's song.) Spencer argues that food and the pleasure derived from it are too closely related to utilitarian functions to be indulged in for their own sakes; they remain intimately connected with satisfaction of physical need. This is less true with other senses, such as hearing and sight. The more the dissociation from usefulness, in the sense of sustaining life, the more a sense impression can be engaged in purely aesthetically, in play rather than work. Schiller makes a similar distinction: the eye and ear involve the requisite aesthetic distance, in contrast to the lower sense of touch.[23]

---

[22] Spencer, "Aesthetic Sentiments," in *Principles of Psychology*, II, 646, 631; Carroll, *Letters*, p. 130.

[23] Spencer, "Aesthetic Sentiments," in *Principles of Psychology*, II, 632; Schiller, p. 126.

Carroll too implies such a differentiation. In spite of the elaborate analogy which may be drawn between physical and mental incorporation, there is something directly utilitarian (life-serving) about feeding the body, in contrast with the relaively ineffable, even useless (for practical purposes) feeding of the mind. Carroll draws the contrast in several of his letters to child-friends.

One of his favorite jokes is to offer ink as a substitute for more conventional drinks, as if it were a particularly nice one. In a letter to Amy Hughes he tells the story of three cats who visited him and to each of whom he fed "a spoonful of ink as a treat"—though unfortunately they didn't appreciate it. To Dorothy Joy Lane Poole, Carroll offers the following choice of drink for dinner: "(1) bottled lemonade; (2) ginger-beer; (3) beer; (4) water; (5) milk; (6) vinegar; (7) ink." Ink is the fluid of the mind, the enabler and preserver of thought. It is therefore not surprising that a mental feeder should sometimes become confused in the following manner: What with all of his writing, work, preparation of lectures, marking of papers, says Carroll in a letter to Marion Richards, "sometimes I get *that* confused, I hardly know which is me and which is the inkstand. Pity me, my dear child! The confusion in one's mind doesn't so much matter—but when it comes to putting bread-and-butter, and orange marmalade, into the *inkstand,* and then dipping pens into *oneself,* and filling *oneself* up with ink, you know, it's horrid." Here the analogy between food and ink is clearly set up such that ink becomes Carroll's food and the source from which his pen flows.[24]

In a letter to Dolly Argyles he calls to mind the generally forgotten relationship between a vegetable and a book: "I'm going to send your Papa a little present this Christmas, which

[24] Carroll, *Letters,* undated, pp. 67–68; Nov.11, 1896, pp. 239–240; Oct. 26, 1881, p. 175.

I daresay you may like to look at: it consists of some thin slices of dried vegetables that somebody has found a way of preparing so that it doesn't come to pieces easily: they are marked in a sort of pattern with some chemical stuff or other, and fastened between sheets of pasteboard to preserve them. I believe the *sort* of thing isn't a new invention, but the markings of these are quite new. I inserted them myself."[25] Here writing a book becomes an ingenious and original way of preparing a food substance, making of a vegetable truly food for the mind.

In spite of the analogies and crossovers that Carroll establishes between physical and mental food, he often shows a kind of disdain for actual food, in that it is so tied to physical need and utility. The same may be said for work, which is also fundamentally utilitarian, insofar as it is undertaken only for its life-serving function. In a letter to May Forshall he asks, "Do you ever play at games? Or is your idea of life 'breakfast, lessons, dinner, lessons, tea, lessons, bed, lessons, breakfast, lessons,' and so on? It is a very neat plan of life, and almost as interesting as being a sewing-machine or a coffee-grinder." The adult equivalent of lessons is work proper: "office hours—which I suppose reduce most men to the mental condition of a coffee-mill or a mangle."[26]

A mechanism is what a human organism amounts to when it eats or when it works to eat. As these passages suggest, a life of eating and work alone would be merely a life of service to the animal mechanism (reflecting an antispiritual and materialistic philosophy which Carroll would have been as glad to able to reject as he was a strict godless evolutionism). But when "useless" play is added, life is freed from necessity and becomes humanly interesting.

Carroll often hints at his preference for mental feeding for

[25] Carroll, *Letters*, Jan. 3, 1869, p. 57.
[26] Carroll, *Letters*, March 6, 1879, p. 123; *Sylvie and Bruno Concluded*, illus. Harry Furniss (London, 1893), pp. 1–2.

its own sake over eating to live and shows how the one can be substituted for the other. "Feeding the Mind" concludes by comparing the healthy ability to digest a bun at any time of the day to the same ability with regard to a book, a treatise, "a mental bun, in fact" (FM, p. 31). This comparison—book/ bun—turns up elsewhere in Carroll's writing. But it becomes a matter of a book or a bun, as may be especially well seen in *A Tangled Tale*.

A Tangled Tale—A Book or a Bun?

A Tangled Tale (1885) is a curious hybrid of mathematics and narrative, divided into ten Knots, each a separate word problem in itself, each carrying forward the story of one of three sets of characters: a young traveler named Norman and his aged companion; Clara and her aunt, Mad Mathesis; and Hugh and Lambert and their tutor, Balbus. The latter two sets are tied together in the last Knot, since they turn out to be members of the same household. But the narrative poses a kind of puzzle for the reader: How do Norman and his elderly companion link with the rest of the characters? They must be the older brother and the father of the family, though this is inferrable only: for example, the elder traveler has mentioned his mathematically inclined sister—can this be Mad Mathesis?—and the last scene lets us know there are three sons of the house, two identified as Hugh and Lambert—can the third be Norman? In any event, the mysterious travelers conform to the same principle of pairing found in each of the other groups of characters. There is a puzzle-poser, the older of the two, and a mentally harrassed and struggling puzzle-solver, the younger, who is undergoing arduous training in a game approach to experience.

Knot I sets a pattern. Two travelers, characterized by archaic dress and archaic English to match (both easily shed in later Knots involving the travelers where setting dictates something else—realistic consistency doesn't count for much in the *Tale*) are clambering through a romantic mountain landscape. Carroll establishes a scene and situation out of which a problem can cleverly emerge within two or three pages. He tells us that the younger traveler is "bounding from crag to crag"; the elder, who is weaker in romance but stronger in computation, estimates their pace at "four miles in the hour . . . not an ounce more . . . and not a farthing less!" From the raw materials of what seemed at first a costume adventure piece, the old man concocts a problem: Given that the travelers have spent from three till nine walking along a level road, up a hill, and home again; that their pace on the level is four miles per hour, uphill three mph, downhill six mph; find the distance walked and the time of reaching the hill's summit. To this query, "A groan was the young man's only reply," which, along with convulsed features and furrowed brow, "revealed the abyss of arithmetical agony into which one chance question had plunged him" (*Works*, pp. 983–984).[27]

Repeatedly, *A Tangled Tale* wraps up such arithmetical word problems in entertaining situations involving peculiar characters. Carroll often stresses the incongruity between the exotica of a situation and the prosaica of the characters' response. Knot VI, for example, finds the travelers landed upon a tropical island where reigns a plump little queen who is addressed as Her Radiancy, Her Serence Brilliance, Her Condensed Milkiness, and who complacently expects everyone, like grasshoppers in a volcano, to be "shrivelled up in the presence of Her Spangled Vehemence." This monarch poses a problem to the travelers, who are meanwhile subsisting in the dungeon on bread and water. The problem is not of the usual romantic sort, to retrieve a magic ring or to make a bewitched princess wake or smile or dance. Instead it is the following: Lolo,

[27] Carroll, *A Tangled Tale*, *Works*, pp. 983–1078; references to *A Tangled Tale* appearing in the text are to this edition; where the illustrations become important I will refer to another edition.

Mimi, and Zuzu, competitors for the post of Imperial Scarf-maker, are to be judged by rate of work, lightness of scarves, and warmth. How do they rank? "Lolo makes 5 scarves while Mimi makes 2; but Zuzu makes four while Lolo makes 3! Again, so fairylike is Zuzu's handiwork, 5 of her scarves weigh no more than one of Lolo's; yet Mimi's is lighter still—5 of hers will but balance 3 of of Zuzu's! And for warmth one of Mimi's is equal to 4 of Zuzu's; yet one of Lolo's is as warm as 3 of Mimi's!" And so on (*Works*, pp. 1004–1005). Fortunately, Carroll's Appendix provides the solution for those of us who are not up to the problem (order of merit = M, L, Z).

Carroll gives another amusing tilt to *A Tangled Tale* by sometimes so arranging reality that it can be conveniently translated into a word problem. The outlines of a problem set in Knot III are summarized in the Appendix in the dry form reminiscent of many a humorless textbook: "Two travelers, starting at the same time, went opposite ways round a circular railway. Trains start each way every 15 minutes, the easterly ones going round in 3 hours, the westerly in 2. How many trains did each meet on the way, not counting trains met at the terminus itself?" (*Works*, p. 1035). The fuzziness that normal reality would introduce into this neat scheme is that the trains would lose an indeterminate number of minutes each time they stopped. But Carroll takes care of that and takes care of any residue of dryness in his Knot at the same time. He invents springboards that catapult passengers into and out of the trains in exactly one second, so that we get a lovely picture: "Two trains rushed into the station. A moment's pause, and they were gone again; but in that brief interval several passengers had been shot into them, each flying straight to his place with the accuracy of a Minie bullet—while an equal number were showered out upon the side-platforms" (*Works*, p. 992). *A Tangled Tale* gives us a word problem world. Nothing escapes; everything can be converted into a puzzle game.

Carroll tells us his intention—to embody in each Knot, like

medicine in jam, some arithmetical, algebraic, or geometrical question. The "fair readers" of *The Monthly Packet* (in which *A Tangled Tale* originally appeared, beginning in April 1880) were meant to receive "amusement" and "possible edification," but in quite unbalanced proportions (*Works*, p. 982). Indeed, the Appendix admits that the "aim is to entertain rather than to instruct" (*Works*, p. 1060).

Emerging very clearly from *A Tangled Tale* is the fact that any narrative situation can be used to provide data for a guessing game, a mathematical puzzle. The adult figures in the *Tale* all look at life as a data bank perfectly suited to this purpose, and are actively engaged in teaching their younger companions, pupils, nieces, sons, and daughters to do likewise. And they are all teachers of the very highhanded school. Much of the humor of the book resembles that found in chapter eight of *Great Expectations*, in which Mr. Pumblechook greets Pip at breakfast with " 'Seven times nine, boy?' " and keeps the sum running through the entire meal, with the consequence that hungry Pip gets hardly a bite swallowed.[28]

The substitution of the mental pleasures of data and calculation for the physical pleasures of eating is presented in Knot X, entitled "Chelsea Buns." Now, instead of emphasizing the analogy between physical and mental feeding as in "Feeding the Mind," *A Tangled Tale* makes the two into alternatives. Mad Mathesis—an "eccentric old lady [who] never let slip an opportunity of driving her niece into a calculation"—has set Clara a percentage to find. " 'How *can* I tell?' " asks the girl; " 'You can't, of course, without data,' " her aunt replies, " 'but I'm just going to give you—.' " At this point a street-vendors voice, rich and musical, chimes in with an ending to Mad Mathesis' sentence: " 'Give her a Chelsea bun, Miss! That's what most young ladies likes best!' " (*Works*, pp.

[28] Dickens, *Great Expectations*, critical and biographical material by Lauriat Lane, Jr. (New York, 1961), pp. 64–65.

1019–1020). But Mad Mathesis does not believe that young ladies should stop with a preference for mere Chelsea buns. What she is giving Clara is not directly desirable like a bun, which is pleasurable and useful to eat; her data are of no value except as means of reaching an end, the answer to the calculation she has set. At the same time the whole problem, made up of the data and the calculation of the answer, is in a sense an end in itself and without intrinsic or utilitarian value; its only value is that conferred upon it by Mad Mathesis' eccentric interest. Her problem is a sort of game, involving mental rather than physical "amusement." Its mental nutritiousness or "possible edification" is surely incidental, the kind of unaimed-at side effect that Spencer concedes may be generated in play.

Any data, any situation or phenomenon encountered in life, can be turned into a pleasure not too far removed from that produced by devouring a Chelsea bun. But this pleasure is more dissociated from ulterior motive or benefit and is undertaken more purely for its own sake. This particular guessing game involves determining what percentage of the Chelsea pensioners have lost an arm, a leg, an eye, and an ear. Clara's original response to seeing these "weather-beaten heroes" is to exclaim, " 'How very, very sad!' " " 'Sad—but very curious when you come to look at it arithmetically,' was her aunt's less romantic reply" (*Works*, p. 1019). Mad Mathesis can transform the sad into the curious simply by making disabilities into data, and data can be manipulated to form an interesting abstract pattern. The veterans are reduced to input for a system to be constructed for its own, and one's own, certainly not for their own sake.

The imagery of another scene in Knot X makes explicit this important motif running through *A Tangled Tale*: the substitution of mental abstraction, calculation, numbers, and especially money for physical nourishment. Clara, Hugh, and Lambert have been called in to their father's study, along with Mad

Mathesis and Balbus. There they find: "Writing materials had been arranged round the table, after the fashion of a ghostly banquet; the butler had evidently bestowed much thought on the grim device. Sheets of quarto paper, each flanked by a pen on one side and a pencil on the other, represented the plates—penwipers did duty for rolls of bread—while ink-bottles stood in the places usually occupied by wine-glasses. The pièce de résistance was a large green baise bag, which gave forth, as the old man restlessly lifted it from side to side, a charming jingle, as of innumerable gold guineas" (*Works*, p. 1023).

Here is a complete feast to go with the ink that Carroll characteristically offers for drink. The whole layout is called "grim." Apparently this feast is just as uninviting as was the spoonful of ink that Carroll gave his three cat guests "as a treat" in the whimsical narrative recounted in the letter to Amy Hughes. After all, as any practical eater might reflect, "If . . . all the sea were ink . . . what *should* we have to drink?"[29] But the teachers in *A Tangled Tale* display an exaggerated and comical disdain for such animal-like practicality, which they aim to demolish; it inhibits one's ability to enjoy play for play's sake.

The bag of guineas standing in for the main course is the prize offered for figuring out the answer to the father's guessing game. The data of the problem, abstracted from his muddled presentation, are as follows: At first two of the sons' ages were equal to that of the third. A few years later, two of them together amounted to double the third. When the number of years since the first occasion equals the sum of the ages on that occasion, one age is twenty-one. Triumphantly the father concludes, " 'Now, my boys, calculate your ages

[29] This traditional nursery rhyme is found as n. 2 to "A Hemispherical Problem," *Works*, p. 1238, rprt. from "Difficulties No. 1," *The Rectory Umbrella* (c. 1850–1853), republished as *The Rectory Umbrella and Mischmasch*, foreword Florence Milner (London, Toronto, Melbourne, Sydney, 1932), n. 3, pp. 31–32.

from the data and you shall have the money!' " (*Works*, pp. 1023–1024).

Hugh's response is the (futile) resistance of one who is not yet a confirmed game player; he objects to the uselessness and circularity of the whole enterprise: " 'But we know our ages!' " he says. Of course that has nothing to do with it. The father is indignant. With tottering steps he drags off the money. His parting dictum is, " 'You must use the data only!' " The problem solvers are disallowed any extra assumptions. For instance, they must even hypothesize ignorance of which son has actually come of age. This requirement of a purely fictional ignorance makes more patent and more galling the arbitrariness of the task they have been set. Left alone with the data. Hugh, Lambert, and Clara are in despair (as so too the readers, then and now, must be meant to be, thus abruptly left to deal with the problem on their own). The three are "crushed . . . with a load of unfathomable mystery." Their despair derives not from lack of the answer, which in fact they already know, but from lack of knowing how to get to it via the points provided (*Works*, pp. 1024–1025).

Carroll repeatedly sets up a relationship between food and money, which is an abstract equivalent of sorts. Nothing is merely to be experienced in *A Tangled Tale*, but must be written down and thereby kept account of. For example, in Knot VII Clara is obliged, after eating her lunch, to itemize it in a notebook with the amount to the penny spent on each item. Apparently, what is converted into a language (words or numbers) is a source of satisfaction—giving one a sense of mental mastery (systemization and permanent command of the facts). Mad Mathesis laments that Clara must drink lemonade at all, instead of plain water as she herself does. Mad Mathesis has other less animal pleasures than lemonade, which Clara must be taught to cultivate, for instance, by keeping up her luncheon "petty cash" accounts. And according to Mad Mathesis, " 'petty cash . . . is a form of pleasure, whatever *you* may think' " (*Works*, p. 1007). Mad Mathesis maintains these accounts just for the pleasure of it. Surely such account keeping is in the nature of play, though poor Clara doesn't find it much fun at first. Asked to itemize her lunch bill on the basis of totals for previous meals, "her mind was a blank, and all human expression was rapidly fading out of her face" (*Works*, p. 1011). Mad Mathesis has a different definition of what's human from Clara, but Clara is learning.

Much of *A Tangled Tale* goes to show how any phenomenon can be divested of intrinsic meaning or value and converted to data which are meaningful and valuable only in terms of a game system. For example, Knot V is entitled "Oughts and Crosses," which, as Carroll remarks in the Appendix, is "a very old game" (*Works*, p. 1045). The terms of this game are paintings at Burlington House, divided into paintings exhibiting three attributes: choice of subject, arrangement, and coloring. All other qualities that a painting might have, no matter how affecting they might be to the viewer, are entirely irrelevant. The rules are: " 'You must give three crosses to two or three pictures. You must give two crosses to four or five. . . . And you must give one cross to nine or ten.' " What constitutes winning, Clara wants to know. She learns that the object is to mark the fewest possible pictures, giving three oughts to one or two pictures, two to three or four, one to eight or nine. Clara is overwhelmed by the complexity of this game. But she is nevertheless "determined to win." As they begin with a portrait of Lieutenant Brown mounted on his favorite elephant, Mad Mathesis shows like determination with a grim smile. Games may be for pleasure, but they are not for that reason laughing matters.[30] One is out to beat the enemy.

What happens is that Clara's standards and indeed her

[30] Play and seriousness need not be antithetical at all according to Huizinga, p. 18.

whole way of seeing the paintings end up being dictated by the game. Once entering into a game in order to master its system and one's opponent, one voluntarily limits and circumscribes one's perspective and behavior. Compare this observation of Carroll's in a letter to Marion Richards: "Now I come to think of it, *do* we decide questions at all? We decide *answers* no doubt; but surely the questions decide us?"[31] After a time spent in marking, Clara surprises the two little old ladies by telling them how desperately she needs to find a picture " 'that has a good subject—and that's well arranged—but badly coloured.' " The questions set by the game are here deciding what answers Clara desires to find. The ladies try to pacify her. They ask her what the subject is of the particular painting she seems bent on locating. " 'You know it doesn't matter a bit what the subject *is*, so long as it's a good one!' " answers Clara. The two ladies, of course, cannot understand such standards; they aren't in on the game (*Works*, p. 1000). Clara is acting perfectly rationally in terms of her system, but equally rationally, the old ladies fear she may be mad. The rationality of any one game system or universe may be complete, but it is strictly limited to its own mental enclosure.

The beginning of Knot II shows how for the inveterate game player every phenomenon is assumed to be rationalizable, capable of integration into some clear mental system. The tutor Balbus (named after the central figure of Hugh's and Lambert's Latin textbook) does not see the sentences in the textbook merely as exercises in grammatical form, and therefore according to any other criterion, quite random, arbitrary, and really nonsensical. No, Balbus seeks a principle which will make these sentences part of a more inclusively coherent order. He insists on interpreting each one as the vehicle for a moral point, so that all together the sentences would amount to a moral code. Thus the sentence, "Balbus has overcome all his

---

[31] Carroll, *Letters*, Feb. 8, 1886, p. 178.

enemies," is interpreted by the tutor to mean "Successful Bravery." "Balbus has borrowed a healthy dragon" equals "Rashness in Speculation" (*Works*, p. 985).

A charming drawing in the book version of *A Tangled Tale* of 1885, illustrated by Arthur Frost, shows how "Balbus was assisting his mother-in-law to convince the dragon," which presumably points the moral "Influence of Sympathy in United Action."[32] For Balbus this system is plausible, reasonably consistent, and not self-contradictory; it therefore satisfies him. Coherence and symmetry are aesthetic pleasures. Knot II shows Balbus exalted into a "dream of beauty" by the contemplation of the very squareness of the town square: " 'Beautiful! Beau-ti-ful! Equilateral! *And* rectangular! . . . Twenty doors on a side! What symmetry! . . . It's delicious!' " (*Works*, pp. 986–987).

In Knot IX the tutor formulates a plausible argument with a wonderfully improbable conclusion: "If you hold a stick, six feet long, with its ends in a tumbler of water, and wait long enough, you must eventually be immersed." Of course a tumbler would run out of water before the immersion point; so Balbus postulates a stick held in the sea (very nicely illustrated). The conclusion now appears to flow inevitably from the accepted premise that if a solid is partially immersed in water, it displaces an amount of water equal to the amount of immersed solid. This water, he reasons, must rise, hence immersing more of the solid, hence causing the water to rise again, and so on and on. "It is self-evident that this process must continue till the entire solid [the stick] is immersed, and that the liquid will then begin to immerse whatever holds the solid [the man]" (*Works*, p. 1018).

Just as Balbus had been obliged, according to his system of moralization of Latin texts, to translate the all but ethically inert statement, "Balbus, having scorched the tail of the dragon,

[32] Carroll, *A Tangled Tale*, illus. Arthur B. Frost (London, 1885), p. 6.

went away," into a moral dictum, "Prudence" (*Works*, p. 985), so must he conclude in a systematic fashion that the man at the sea's edge who bravely holds on to the end of a stick must eventually be drowned. Balbus is so convinced by his reasoning that he even claims empirical evidence as verification of his deductive proof: "The multitudes who daily perish in this manner to attest a philosophical truth, and whose bodies the unreasoning wave casts sullenly upon our thankless shores, have a truer claim to be called the martyrs of science than a Galileo or a Kepler!' " Balbus suspects a fallacy somewhere, but it doesn't bother him enough to keep him awake. He has reached closure, a sense of mental mastery, with the grateful relaxation that follows after. "He closed his eyes, in order to concentrate his attention more perfectly, and for the next hour or so his slow and regular breathing bore witness to the careful deliberation with which he was investigating this new and perplexing view of the subject" (*Works*, p. 1018).

Lambert doesn't care either about testing the relationship between a given scientific theory and the real world. To apply what Jean Piaget tells us, such experimental testing would be appropriate to accommodation, but not to incorporation or logical and mathematical deduction. It must be said that Hugh (the same brother who objects that he knows his age when asked to find it out by a torturous method) does briefly resist on empirical grounds Balbus' assertion that if a body is immersed in a liquid, it displaces liquid equal to its own bulk. When he puts a little bucket into a big one containing water, things don't seem to turn out that way (because of an ambiguity in the meaning of the word "displaces," as Carroll scrupulously explains in the Appendix, *Works*, p. 1066).[33] But

[33] Carroll explains the fallacy in Balbus' water-displacing theory (Appendix, *Works*, p. 1067): there is no authority for assuming that, if water rises in a series of installments having no end, there is no limit to the level to which it can rise. He illustrates: "This series [e.g., a rise of water level

Lambert's response is, " 'If Balbus says it's the same bulk, why it *is* the same bulk, you know' " (*Works*, p. 1015). Here we have the stolid faith of the ordinary game player, who never questions the givens, as to do so would destroy the game.

In *A Tangled Tale* Carroll stands in the same relationship to the reader as Balbus to his pupils, Mad Mathesis to her niece, the older traveler to the younger Norman. In the Appendix he answers the problems Knot by Knot with a rating and commentary on the solutions that had been sent in by readers of *The Monthly Packet*. Those who were wrong or partially wrong—and not many were fully right—he chides on some of the same grounds for which the young problem solvers of the *Tale* are chided. A solution rates low with him if it does not include the working out. The method is as important or more important than the answer itself. One must not only get to the end but complete the circle, touching all appropriate points. Carroll repeatedly admonishes respondents for indulging in unwarranted assumptions, not sticking to the data. Those who guess or work with numbers picked on a hunch are called malefactors and sternly lowered to places far down on the "Class List." They are short-circuiting the problem.

One reader wrote in to complain about the "very trenchant expressions" Carroll used in criticizing the answers submitted. Carroll responds that any severe language he might have written was meant in jest, not at all to annoy, for language likely to annoy would be unjustified no matter how wrong the other person, how correct himself (*Works*, pp. 1063–1064). Still it is clear from his tone in the Appendix and from the tones of the problem posers in the *Tale* itself (especially Mad Mathesis, who is forever "terrifying" Clara with her relentless questioning) that setting a puzzle—the presumption being that one can answer it oneself—gives one an upper hand, a

in such a progression as: 2″, 1″, ½″, etc.] can never reach 4 inches, since, however many terms we take, we are always short of 4 inches by an amount equal to the last term taken."

psychological advantage, and can even amount to bullying. The logic and mathematics in this book are not tailored for enabling one to get on in practical life. Rather *A Tangled Tale* dramatizes the way that any set of circumstances can be converted into data and made the basis for a contest. Almost every episode illustrates some form of mental browbeating. For that matter, the whole constitutes the material for a contest between its readers, and virually all of these readers are in the position of being browbeaten by Carroll.[34] As he suggests in a letter to his child-friend Gaynor Simpson, a riddle is used, maybe mainly used, to "triumph" over those who must struggle to solve it. Likewise, the problems in *Symbolic Logic* offer "opportunity, gentle Reader, for playing a trick on your innocent friend."[35]

Beyond "edification," *A Tangled Tale* conveys "amusement" of a special and heady kind. In February 1887, a young man inscribed a copy of the *Tale* with this very Victorian, facetious, but accurate estimate of its potential value for his sisters: "For my four little sisters—to raise the intellectual standard of the schoolroom ["possible edification"] and *to enable them to be the terror of their neighbors* ["amusement"]" (italics mine). Carroll knew well enough what terrorizing one's neighbors could mean. Games are not so to say all fun and games. In a letter to Helen Feildon he recalls a scene that must have been familiar enough, and we may sympathize with the poor child interrupted at her dinner with food for the mind:

> I must tell you an awful story of my trying to set a puzzle to a little girl the other day. It was at a dinner party, at

[34] Carroll frequently had to excuse or explain away his browbeating in the course of his correspondence with child-friends. Such statements are typical: "Really you musn't begin to believe my letters to be all meant seriously, or I shall be so frightened I shan't dare to write to you"; and, "Please tell Jessie I meant it *all* for nonsense." Letters to Agnes Hull, Dec. 18, 1879, and to Sallie Sinclair, Feb. 9, 1878, *Letters*, pp. 144, 156.

[35] Carroll, *Letters*, undated, p. 91; *Symbolic Logic*, p. 69.

dessert. I had never seen her before, but, as she was sitting next me, I rashly proposed to her to try the puzzle (I daresay you know it) of "the fox, and goose, and bag of corn." And I got some biscuits to represent the fox and the other things. Her mother was sitting on the other side, and said, "Now mind you take pains, my dear, and do it right!" The consequences were awful; She *shrieked* out "I can't do it! I can't do it! Oh Mamma! Mamma!" threw herself into her mother's lap, and went off into a fit of sobbing which lasted several minutes! That was a lesson to me about trying children with puzzles. I do hope the square window [another puzzle—Carroll didn't reform after his lesson] won't produce any awful effects on *you!*[36]

In a typical half-charming, half-cutting letter, Carroll wrote to Marion Richards about *A Tangled Tale*, revealing his awareness of the strange substitute nature of the book's amusement value. He wonders whether she "will get most pleasure from the fiction in this little book, or pain from the problems" (depending on whether she masters them or they her). As for the relative merit of what pleasure there is, it is not at all certain that the mental would always be preferred to the physical: Carroll wonders "whether you will feel satisfaction at the thought that your ancient friend yet remembers you, or dissatisfaction at finding he has so far forgotten your tastes as to send you a book instead of a bun."[37]

In a letter to Nellie Knight, Carroll expresses the same quandary: whether he really ought to send her "a Chelsea Bun, or a Book!" The not very flattering implication in both letters is

---

[36] Inscription dated Feb. 1887, and signed "Allen," written on the flyleaf of the University of California, Berkeley, copy of *A Tangled Tale*, illus. Arthur B. Frost (London, 1885); Carroll, March 15, 1873, in Collingwood, ed., *Diversions and Digressions*, pp. 214–215.

[37] Carroll, *Letters*, Feb. 8, 1886, p, 178.

that Carroll is not quite sure whether the recipient is a baby who equates pleasure with food, or whether she is up to the more advanced but dangerous (because combative and involving possible defeat) pleasures of the mind.[38]

Do you want a book or a bun? Are you an infant, an animal, or a human being? Life is no more than mechanical so long as it consists only of eating, lessons, work. When it rises above such purposes as are dictated by necessity, when out of its own spirit it creates purposes of its own, from nothing and no matter how silly—and in *A Tangled Tale* and elsewhere they are pointedly silly—then it plays and is human. And as we see already, playing means, for Carroll, playing games.

[38] Carroll, *Letters*, Sept. 1, 1888, p. 209. Ruth Gamlen, for example, found Carroll's (Dodgson's) anxiety that she should play one of his elaborate games (probably *Symbolic Logic*) "the beginning of the end." It was too much for her, and he subsequently dropped their friendship; see "By Mrs. A. T. Waterhouse (née Ruth Gamlen) Appendix A, II," Hudson, p. 318.

2. Games

Carroll's Games

Lewis Carroll (Charles Dodgson) was a game player, and he published many games, for the most part under his pseudonym or anonymously. Here is a list of some of his published games and treatises on games:

Rules for Court Circular (1860; second edition, 1862)

Croquet Castles (1863; second edition, 1866)

Puzzles from Wonderland (1870)

A Charade (1878)

Word-Links (1878, an early version of Doublets)

Doublets (1879; abridged edition, 1879; second edition, 1880; third edition, 1880)

A Game for Two Players (1879, an early form of Lanrick)

Lanrick (1881)

Mischmasch (1882)

Letters to *The St. James Gazette* on "Lawn Tennis Tournaments" (August 12, 1882, and August 1, 4, 21, 1883)

"Lawn Tennis Tournaments: The True Method of Assigning Prizes with a Proof of the Fallacy of the Present Method" (1883)

The Game of Logic (first private edition, 1886; second edition, 1887)

Circular Billiards (1890; different second and third issues)

Syzygies: A Word-Puzzle (in *The Lady*, 1891; reprinted July 30, 1891)

Syzygies and Lanrick (1893; second edition, 1893)

Rules for Co-operative Backgammon (in a letter to *The Times*, March 6, 1894)

One might also include *Symbolic Logic* (1896) in this list; it was after all accompanied by a card, or playing board, and gray and red counters, just as *The Game of Logic* was.[1]

These games reached the public; others were invented or improved for private use. There was Railway Dominoes and a version of chess with an "in statuquo" board for playing on the train. (Carroll habitually carried with him toys and puzzle games; and trains, along with the seaside, were especially suitable places for bringing these out, the better to become acquainted with his favorite friends, little girls.) Another game involves moving letters about on a chessboard until they form words, rather in the manner of what we know as Scrabble. Carroll invented several variations on backgammon. One was called Blot-Backgammon; though the diary tells us little about this game, it seems each player scores the other's points. Thirdie Backgammon calls for the use of three rather than two dice, thus introducing more choice and presumably more need for skill and allowing for the handicapping of the stronger player. Another version, Co-operative Backgammon, complicates things further by stipulating that two of the three dice are thrown for one's own moves, the other for moving the opponent. "Co-operative" is a strange term for the relation between the players here, as they must certainly cooperate in no sense of the word except by their mutual endeavors to set each other back. The game no doubt fits into the long/agonizing category. Arithmetical Croquet also sounds rather painful; Carroll's explanation in a manuscript copy gives some notion of the intricacy of his games:

[1] For descriptions of these games see *The Lewis Carroll Handbook*, a new version of Sidney Herbert Williams and Falconer Madan, *A Handbook of the Literature of the Rev. C. L. Dodgson* (1931), rev. and augmented Roger Lancelyn Green (London, 1962).

1. The first player names a number not greater than 8: the second does the same: the first then names a higher number, not advancing more than 8 beyond his last; and so on alternately—whoever names 100, which is "winning peg," wins the game.

2. The numbers 10, 20, etc. are the "hoops." To "take" a hoop, it is necessary to go, from a number below it, to one the same distance above it. . . . To miss a hoop twice loses the game.

3. It is also lawful to "take" a hoop by playing *into* it, in one turn, and out of it, to the same distance above it in the next turn. . . .

4. Whatever step one player takes, bars the other from taking an equal step, or the difference between it and 9. . . . But a player has no "barring" power when playing *into* a hoop, or when playing from any number between 90 and 100, unless the other player is also at such a number.

5. The "winning-peg," like the "hoops," may be "missed" once, but to miss it twice loses the game.

6. When one player is "in" a hoop, the other can keep him in, by playing the number he needs for coming out, so as to bar him from using it. He can also do it by playing the difference between this and 9. And he may thus go on playing the two barring numbers alternately: but he may not play either twice running.[2]

Unfortunately Carroll has not left an equally generous explanation of another game, apparently of his invention, with the fetching Darwinian name Natural Selection.[3] The competitiveness of Carroll's idea of playing, which figures in all his games, squares with the general theory of life that serves him for a title. Herbert Spencer's comment applies here: "no

[2] Carroll, *Diaries*, II, 463; I, 249; II, 392, 264–265, 508, 509, 314–315.
[3] Carroll, *Diaries*, II, 375.

matter what the game, the satisfaction is in achieving victory—
in getting the better of an antagonist."

Carroll was interested in all sorts of gaming, in a theoretical
way. He was no gambler, but he did submit to the *Pall Mall
Gazette* a rule for making a winning rule in betting. Mostly,
he amused himself with variations upon traditional parlor and
garden games of the sort he often played with child-friends.
One of these, Grace Denman, is captured in a photograph by
Carroll holding her croquet mallet. Regular croquet (including
parlor croquet) and regular backgammon are frequently mentioned in the diaries. According to Isa Bowman, a favorite who
wrote a book about Carroll when she grew up, backgammon
was "a game of which he was passionately fond, and of which
he could never have enough." "Chess," we are told in the
diary entry for September 3, 1866, "is the family occupation
at present." On August 10, Carroll observed a chess tourna-
ment, and his stated preference for consultation games and
his registration of games on official sheets so that they might
be replayed reveal his technical interest. Chess had been a
family occupation before this time; one of Carroll's photographs shows his two aunts playing chess, taken probably in
1858. Nor was it dropped later; Carroll tells us he played
chess on the train during his journey to Russia in 1867.[4]

Other popular games noted in the diaries are halma, nine
men's morris, ways and means, the Ural mountains, haymak-
ing, and many charades. It should be remembered that the
original of "Jabberwocky" was the product of a parlor game

[4] Carroll, *Diaries*, I, 247; Gernsheim, *Lewis Carroll Photographer*, plate
39; Bowman, *The Story of Lewis Carroll, Told for Young People by the
Real Alice in Wonderland* (London, 1900), p. 67; Carroll, *Diaries*, I, 246;
Gernsheim, plate 11; Carroll, "Journal of a Tour in Russia in 1867," in
*The Russian Journal and Other Selections from the Works of Lewis
Carroll*, ed. with introd. John Francis McDermott, 1st ed. (New York,
1935), pp. 85, 114 (first privately published as C. L. Dodgson, *Tour in
1867* [Philadelphia, 1928]).

of verse making played with the Misses Wilcox at Whitburn in 1855.[5]

As for the traditional favorite, cards, Carroll records that he first learned to play in the few days after January 16, 1858, when he bought *Hoyle's Games.* Just nine days later he completed the rules for his own card game of Court Circular.[6]

The museum at the town of Guildford, where Carroll bought a house for his sisters after their father's death, possesses two typical instructional games: a history jigsaw puzzle of William IV's time and a game called The Wheel of Life. These may be from Carroll's own childhood at Croft. Carroll's library at Oxford included, as one might expect, many books of games and puzzles, including Ranjitsinghji's *Jubilee Book of Cricket.* At the sale of his property at the Holywell Music Room, Oxford, on May 10 and 11, 1898, these items, in addition to various clocks, glasses, mathematical and geometrical instruments, and photograph albums, were on the block: a set of chessmen in a case, plus sets of backgammon and draughts.[7]

It has been often enough remarked that Carroll (or Dodgson) lived his life, so to speak, according to *Hoyle.* Florence Becker Lennon says in *Victoria through the Looking-Glass,* "His life was a game, even his logic, his mathematics, and his singular ordering of his household and other affairs. His logic was a game and his games were logical." Such a view of Carroll's logic, which was after all part of the academic discipline that was his work, is corroborated by R. B. Braithwaite in "Lewis Carroll as Logician": "Carroll regarded formal and symbolic logic not as a corpus of systematic knowledge about valid thought nor yet as an art for teaching a person to think correctly, but as a game." Rev. W. Tuckwell, who knew Carroll, states that his "life [was] mapped out in squares like

[5] Hudson, *Lewis Carroll,* p. 81.

[6] Carroll, *Diaries,* I, 138–139.

[7] Guildford Corporation, *Lewis Carroll and Guildford* (Guildford, 1966), p. 2; Hudson, pp. 89, 12, 13.

Alice's landscape." This conclusion seems justified, whether we consider Carroll's elaborate letter-filing system, the puzzle problems he invented to occupy his mind and keep it from painful or forbidden thoughts on sleepless nights, or his extreme punctilio in setting up precise rules concerning which child-friends were and were not kissable (it was an age of profuse kissing, but Carroll learned to regulate such exchanges with precaution, on the basis of the age and modesty of the child-friend, and of the permission, in advance, of the mama). Again, in Lennon's words, "Here was a particularly big person who spent his life fitting himself, with infinite art and patience, and even, as if it were one of his own puzzle games, with a certain amusement, into a particularly small and exactly delimited box." Lennon implies that such a delimitation is somehow deplorable. Fortunately, we need not all deplore the same things. What is important is that Carroll's art expresses a kind of game player's mentality.[8]

We are concerned here with the notion of game as opposed to the more encompassing notion of play. The play of what Piaget calls the third period, from ages seven to eleven and afterward, consist of "games with rules," and these last into adult life because "they are the ludic activity of the socialized being." Rules exist when more than one are playing, for they are meaningless except to regulate interchange or competition, to impose "an idea of obligation which presupposes at least two individuals." They "necessarily imply social or interindividual relationships." (An exception is solitaire, British pa-

[8] Lennon, *Victoria through the Looking-Glass: The Life of Lewis Carroll* (New York, 1945), pp. 169, 8; Braithwaite, "Lewis Carroll as Logician," *Mathematical Gazette*, XVI (July 1932), 174; he also mentions Carroll in his *Theory of Games as a Tool for the Moral Philosopher* (Cambridge, 1955), p. 17; Tuckwell, *Reminiscences Of Oxford* (London, 1900), pp. 161–162, quoted in Hudson, p. 212; Dodgson, "Introduction," *Curiosa Mathematica Part II: Pillow-Problems Thought out during Sleepless Nights* (London, 1893); Hudson, pp. 265–266.

tience, which is structured by analogy to regular rule games; that is, to play solitaire one must have a conception of rules binding on oneself because accepted by a group, and a conception of competition, which is implicitly social, and of winning, in this case over chance rather than a living opponent.) Besides giving us this distinction, Piaget has little to say about games with rules. But Carroll's imaginative universe is overwhelmingly one of rule games—witness *A Tangled Tale*, which is not only about games where one is typically "determined to win," but which itself constitutes a competitive game for the readers.[9]

Of the four types of play categorized by structure in Roger Callois' *Man, Play, and Games,* Carroll's favored type is Agon (competition). All of Callois' types appear to me to have something to do with assertion of control: Mimicry in Freud's sense that simulation is a way of mastering reality, Alea (games of chance) and Ilinz (vertigo play) as perhaps roundabout versions of the same thing—that is, abandoning oneself to a certain loss of control adds to the pleasure, even against the odds of chance and dizziness, of reasserting it. But the sort of mastery found in Carroll's games, the games that go into his imaginative writing, is the obvious "getting-the-better-of-an-antagonist" kind.[10]

Even in *The Game of Logic* Carroll stresses how much greater pleasure is to be derived if two sit down to it together, rather than one alone. While he does not actually say that the two must compete in solving the various syllogisms, this certainly would be the likely pattern. Again, the pleasures of "triumphing" over one's neighbors should be remembered. Virtually all of Carroll's full-fledged games are labeled "for two players" or more. As we are informed by game theory, an essential feature of a game is that there be at least two players each of whom must make choices and receive payoffs. In *Two-*

9 Piaget, *Play, Dreams and Imitation*, pp. 142, 112–113.
10 Callois, *Man, Play, and Games* (New York, 1961).

Person Game Theory Anatol Rapoport also gives the interesting bit of information that a well-known variant of chess is named "Kriegspiel" or "warplay," and *Hoyle* tells us that "backgammon" is Welsh for "little battle." Such names suggest the importance of the fighting element in play.[11]

"Play is battle and battle is play," according to the Germanic attitude, and by the same token, a riddle is precisely a version of the basic *"halsrätsel,"* to be answered or "off with your head." Evidence like this convinces Huizinga that play is basically "agonistic." It is natural enough that the "urge for mastery" should find expression via mastery over others. According to *Homo Ludens:* "We want the satisfaction of having done something well. Doing something well means doing it better than others."[12]

One is on one's own, to master the situation and the opponent. Losing the game is a blow to one's ego, and there is no one to blame but oneself. *Hoyle,* the Bible of the nineteenth-century game player, does not attempt to soften this truism: "If your game is such, that you have scarcely anything to play, it is your own fault, either for having brought out your pieces wrong, or, which is worse, not at all; for had they been brought out right, you must have sufficient variety to play." Karl Groos tells us that board and card games (the basic structuring motifs for the two *Alices*) symbolize physical contests and that pleasure in such activity is "primarily attributable to the combative instinct."[13] If play is combative, it is also at least potentially destructive should the rules fail to hold the contestants within bounds. Games with rules are highly social-

---

[11] Carroll, "Preface," *Game of Logic;* Rapoport, *Two-Person Game Theory: The Essential Ideas* (Ann Arbor, Mich., 1966), pp. 18–21, 63; *Hoyle's Games Containing the Rules for Playing Fashionable Games,* rev. from the last London ed. (New York, 1857), p. 161.

[12] Huizinga, *Homo Ludens,* pp. 40–41, 108, 30–31, 63; for Huizinga, "Contest means play," p. 76.

[13] *Hoyle,* pp. 214–215; Groos, *Play of Man,* p. 190.

ized structures of controlled antagonism. But antagonism is a strong force, and we will see that Carroll was aware of this and disturbed by it, though he never gave up his devotion, his addiction, to games.

Systems: Geometry, Logic, and Language and the Mental Treasure of Certainty

Terms and rules—these are the constituents of a game in Elizabeth Sewell's definition in her book on Carroll (and Lear), *The Field of Nonsense*. Her definition is not fitted to loose make-believe play (Piaget's first stages) but to activities like chess, tennis, crossword puzzles, and so on: "A GAME: the active manipulation, serving no useful purpose, of a certain object or class of objects, concrete or mental, [what I call terms] within a limited sphere of space and time and according to fixed rules, with the aim of producing a given result despite the opposition of chance and/or opponents." This is a workable definition and may be applied to systems, whether they be of mathematics, logic, language, or games proper.[14]

[14] Sewell, *The Field of Nonsense* (London, 1952), p. 27. Elizabeth Sewell is the most prominent critic of Carroll's fiction under the aspect of play. Her thesis is that nonsense is founded on the dichotomy between play and dream, the forces of order and disorder in the mind (to understand which—although I have a hard time being convinced—one almost needs to go to her *The Structure of Poetry* [London, 1951]). There are objections: her claim that nonsense is in the verse, not the prose; her insistence that it must exclude reference to reality, which she feels the *Snark* fails to do and so isn't truly nonsense; her dissociation of play and the aesthetic and play and dream, the continuities between which are emphasized, for example, by Huizinga and Piaget. But the main difference between my approach and hers is that I am concerned with play as a theme in Carroll's fiction; she is concerned with play in a definition of nonsense: *The Field of Nonsense* is a genre study and a provocative one. Its helpfulness to my work lies in its pointing out that play is important in the *Alices*, and in its workable definition of games. Sewell ceases to be

One of the best explanations I know of the appeal of the fixed, articulated universe of the board game is given by T. E. Hulme in his *Speculations*. Conceiving of phenomena as chaos, a heap of cinders, he states the "ideal of knowledge: all cinders reduced to counters (words); these counters moved about on a chess-board, and so all phenomena made obvious"; "Think of a lot of pieces on a draught board. When you are told where the pieces [terms] are, and what moves they make [rules], then the mind is satisfied that it completely understands the phenomena. An omniscient intelligence could know no more about that board than you do."[15]

Sewell claims that language—whether words, or even more successfully, numbers—makes possible the creation of such game universes, since it allows experience to be split into discrete, labeled units. These can then be manipulated by the mind, which arranges and so controls an entire sphere of experience. She corroborates Piaget's idea that mathematics and, in word form, logic constitute assimilative deductive schemes, which, because they can be self-contained, airtight vis-à-vis

---

very helpful where her personal convictions lead her simply to condemn a play-view of life in Carroll: "After all, the universe is not a chessboard, the player is not God, and no human being is allowed to play forever and with everything" (pp. 181–182). Other treatments of Carroll's literature and play are G. K. Chesterton's "Lewis Carroll," in his *A Handful of Authors* (London, New York, 1953), pp. 112–119, which considers nonsense a game, a lark, nonsense for nonsense's sake, on the principle of art for art's sake, and Alfred Liede's *Dichtung als Speil: Studien zur Unsinnspoesie an den Grenzen der Sprache*, 2 vols. (Berlin, 1963), I, 25–26, 115–165, which considers the function of the nonsense genre as an escape, a holiday, mere play, in overearnest, repressive Victorian society. Jean Gattegno's *Lewis Carroll* (Paris, 1970), pp. 208–212, 353–361, shows how a game attitude to reality allows us to make up and control our own worlds, and relates this biographically to Carroll.

[15] Hulme, "The Philosophy of Intensive Manifolds" and "Cinders," in *Speculations: Essays on Humanism and the Philosophy of Art*, ed. Herbert Read, frontispiece and foreword Jacob Epstein, 2d ed. (London, 1936), pp. 176, 230.

the reality which might demand accommodation, are therefore highly satisfying to the ego's desire for mastery by incorporation. Here is what Carroll says on this subject in the Preface to *Curiosa Mathematica: Part I* (1888) : "It may well be doubted whether, in all the range of Science, there is any field so fascinating to the explorer—so rich in hidden treasures—so fruitful in delightful surprises—as that of Pure Mathematics. The charm lies chiefly, I think, in the absolute *certainty* of its results: for that is what, beyond almost all mental treasures, the human intellect craves for. Let us only be sure of *something*."[16] Carroll finds the mental treasure of certainty painfully elusive, even in the relatively controllable systems of mathematics and geometry. In later passages in *Curiosa Mathematica*, he must, with regret, confess that there exist certain theorems which are only approximately true.[17]

Carroll is concerned, in *Euclid and His Modern Rivals* (1879), with the relativity of what he calls "axiomaticity"; he expresses the wish that we had units as definitive, say, as inches, by which to measure it (*EMR*, II, vi, 1, p. 129).[18] This geometrical treatise in whimsical dramatic form fulfills Carroll's earlier statement in his diary that an interesting collection might be made of Euclid's tacitly assumed axioms.[19] For example, Carroll's spokesman in *Euclid and His Modern Rivals*, the geometry Professor Minos, though he is the defender of

[16] Sewell, p. 29; Dodgson, *Curiosa Mathematica Part I: A New Theory of Parallels* (London, 1888), p. ix.

[17] For instance, one of his own axioms (that "in any Circle the inscribed Hexagon is greater than any of the segments that lie outside it") is an appeal to the eye rather than to the reason. But then, he tells us, so are those foundation axioms of Euclid's: "Two straight lines cannot enclose a space," and "All right angles are equal"; see Dodgson, *Curiosa Mathematica Part I*, pp. xiv–xv.

[18] Dodgson, *Euclid and His Modern Rivals*, 2d ed. (London, 1885); hereafter identified in the text as *EMR*, with act, scene, section (when applicable), and page reference.

[19] Carroll, *Diaries*, Nov. 15, 1862, I, 189.

Euclid, still notes that Euclid must sometimes appeal to nothing more certain than "the depths of your own consciousness—assuming such depths to exist" in order, for example, to establish the difference between curved and straight lines (*EMR*, I, ii, 5, p. 43). He observes another form of the relativity of axiomaticity: "What is an Axiom at one stage of our knowledge is often anything but an Axiom at an earlier stage" (*EMR*, I, ii, 5, p. 40). If time as well as intuition affect what is an axiom, the system of which it is a foundation cannot offer that fixity and absoluteness which Carroll identifies as the most desirable of mental treasures.

The biggest stumbling block to the stability and certainty of the Euclidian universe, and the one which in fact finally disrupted it, producing non-Euclidian geometry and a radically different mode of conceiving space, is the theory of parallel lines. Carroll does not shirk this topic in *Euclid and His Modern Rivals;* he attempts to back up Euclid, primarily on the grounds that in spite of "some mysterious flaw [that] lies at the root of our subject," Euclid still succeeds in making the very shaky and uncertain axiom concerning parallel lines "a little more axiomatic" than any of his rivals is able to do, and in addition, more concise and less of a strain upon the faith of the reader (*EMR*, I, ii, 5, pp. 42, 44, 46; II, iv, pp. 68–69).

Minos scorns any attempt to argue from the observed consequences of an assumed axiom (*EMR*, II, v, pp. 80–81)—recall Balbus' disdain of empirical verification. Presumably such empiricism would be a humiliating and probably unreliable accommodation, inappropriate in the pure sphere (or what Carroll would have liked to be a pure sphere) of beautifully self-contained, gratifyingly self-consistent, and logical geometry.

Euclid and His Modern Rivals makes clear that an act of pure unsupported faith is necessary to establish axioms, from which all else follows. It is a question what things we might believe if we tried (and what strange conclusions might in due course proceed). In one of the earliest surviving letters to a child-friend, Carroll raises this question in humorous form. He relates to Mary Macdonald the visit of the Bishop of Oxford, on which occasion Carroll threw a book at his head; the following memorandum is then attached:

> Mem: this isn't quite true—so you needn't believe it— Don't be in such a hurry to believe next time—I'll tell you why—If you set to work to believe everything, you will tire out the muscles of your mind, and then you won't be able to believe the simplest true things. Only last week a friend of mind set to work to believe Jack-the-giant-killer. He managed to do it, but he was so exhausted by it that when I told him it was raining (which was true) he *couldn't* believe it, but rushed out into the street without his hat or umbrella, the consequence of which was his hair got seriously damp, and one curl didn't recover its right shape for nearly two days. (Mem: some of *that* is not quite true, I'm afraid—).[20]

Euclid, like God (and like Jack-the-giant-killer?), requires a leap. Probabilities are all Carroll claims in geometry (*EMR*, I, ii, 5, p. 42), and in religion too, for that matter. In a letter addressed to an agnostic, Carroll defends Christianity on the basis that it is internally consistent and that "the probabilities are enormous that the theory is true: & enormous probabilities are what we live by." But "I have a deep dread of argument on religious topics," he writes to Edith Rix. This is understandable since, citing his diary and another letter, logic or no logic, "My vew of life is, that it's next to impossible to convince *anybody* of *anything*" because "one of the hardest things in the world is to convey a meaning accurately from one mind to another."[21]

[20] Carroll, *Letters*, May 23, 1864, pp. 22–23.

[21] Carroll, "Draft for a Letter to an Agnostic," *Diaries*, II, 571; Carroll, letter to Edith Rix, Jan. 15, 1886, diary entry Feb. 20, 1890, and letter to Dora Abdy, 1896, quoted in Collingwood, *Life and Letters*, pp. 251, 291,

If mathematics itself, the language of numbers, is so little reliable for the construction of a flawless mental world which is dependable for communication, how much less so that language of words, even in its most formally controlled aspect, logic.

The Game of Logic and *Symbolic Logic* are intended in part to show up the abysmal illogic which passes for thinking in normal life. They do so, but they also expose the unnerving fact that logicians do not themselves agree on what is logical.[22] It turns out that logicality depends on which system you choose to believe in. Carroll has no desire to enter into controversy with logicians who operate according to their own quite separate arrangements; that is their prerogative, no matter how little we approve, no matter what the consequences: "Let us not quarrel with them, dear Reader! There is room enough in the world for both of us. Let us quietly take our broader system: and, if they choose to shut their eyes . . . we can but stand aside, and let them Rush upon their Fate!" (*GL*, p. 36).[23]

Carroll's own procedure is to present not a series of facts, but a series of agreements for the reader to enter into (*GL*, pp. 5, 37). He proposes certain "universes." These encompass all members of a certain class, which may be imagined as occupying each "cupboard," or square on the board (which is very like a playing board); a counter is used to signal such occupation (or nonoccupation). So we might have a "Universe of Cakes" a "Universe of Lizards," a "Universe of Hornets." ("Wouldn't *that* be a charming Universe to live in?" *GL*, pp. 6–7). And just because a particular universe is not known on

---

331. These reservations about the possibility of convincing others may have entered into Dodgson's decision not to take full holy orders, which would have involved preaching and the care of souls.

[22] Carroll, *Diaries*, Dec. 21, 1893, II, 504.

[23] Carroll, *Game of Logic;* hereafter identified in the text as *GL*, with page reference.

our planet, says Carroll, this does not disqualify it from possible existence on some other. For example, in the case of the "Universe of Dragons," he reminds us: "Remember, I don't guarantee the Premises to be *facts*. In the first place, I never even saw a Dragon: and, in the second place, it isn't of the slightest consequence to us, as *Logicians*, whether our Premisses are true or false: all *we* have to make out is whether they *lead logically to the Conclusion*, so that, if *they* were true, *it* would be true also" (*GL*, p. 25).

All that is needed, as *Symbolic Logic*, like *The Game of Logic*, shows, is clarity of disposition: "I maintain that every writer may adopt his own rule, provided of course that it is consistent with itself and with the accepted facts of logic" (which, as already noted, vary according to logician).[24]

As in *Euclid and His Modern Rivals*, an objection based on experience or consequences bears very little weight. It is outside the game and must simply be left outside. In a strong restatement of his conviction that a logical system is an artificial, not to say arbitrary construct, Carrol repudiates those logicians who in their humility and deference to an impressive abstraction lose sight of the fact that it is their own creature, to be defined and shaped by their fiat:

> The writers, and editors, of the Logical text-books which run in the ordinary grooves . . . take on this subject ["The 'Existential Import of Propositions' "], what seems to me to be a more humble position than is at all necessary. They speak of the Copula of a Proposition "with bated breath," almost as if it were a living, conscious Entity, capable of declaring for itself what it chose to mean and that we, poor human creatures, had nothing to do but to ascertain *what* was its sovereign will and pleasure, and submit to it. In opposition to this view, I main-

[24] Carroll, "Appendix Addressed to Teachers," *Symbolic Logic*, pp. 164–165.

tain that any writer of a book is fully authorized in attaching any meaning he likes to any word or phrase he intends to use. . . . I meekly accept his ruling, however injudicious I may think it.[25]

Above all, one must guard against a propensity toward shiftiness in the terms and rules which in all their different shades of certainty and probability structure the mental system. These are "shadowy and liable to be shifted hither and thither according to the fancies and prejudices of each individual mind" (for instance, the reader's) unless controlled with a strong hand, and unless this control is made binding for other people who enter by their own choosing into the mental realm of the given finite system.[26]

As Elizabeth Sewell says, "Each game . . . is an enclosed whole, with its own rigid laws which cannot be questioned within the game itself; if you put yourself inside the system which is the game, you bind yourself by that system's laws, and so incidentally obtain that particular sense of freedom that games have to offer."[27] In other words, the main thing is to fix the perimeter and the internal relationship structure, the terms and rules, of a game system, and make these stick. Then the universe will be secure (what Carroll calls certain), and one will enjoy the freedom of that security.

It follows, of course, that Carroll is a meticulous, a zealous definer. In *Euclid and His Modern Rivals* Minos laments that because of the multiplication of rival geometries he has not that certainty of his system in scoring papers that a billiard marker would enjoy in scoring a game (*EMR*, I, i, p. 4). Minos objects, for instance, to the fact that in the geometry text of one of his modern rivals, axioms and definitions are scattered through-

---

[25] *Ibid.*, pp. 163–164, and see his castigation of such humility as, for instance, "a *morbid* dread of Negative Attributes," p. 169.

[26] Dodgson, *Curiosa Mathematica, Part I*, pp. xv–xvi.

[27] Sewell, pp. 25–26.

out and unindexed at that (*EMR*, III, i, 5, p. 175). Hence they fail in their function of making things clear from the start, so as to avoid confusion later on. Carroll's own edition of *Euclid, Books I and II* (1882), on the other hand, is admirably definitive. In fact, Carroll inclines to be overdefinitive, as has been pointed out in D. B. Eperson's "Lewis Carroll—Mathematician." In *Notes on Euclid* (1860), Eperson says that Carroll "out-Euclids Euclid by defining the terms 'problem' and 'theorem': 'problem is something to be done,' whilst 'a theorem is something to be believed, for which proof is given.' " He remarks that the process of defining terms can be carried overfar; for example, why not define definition, and so on?[28]

In *Euclid and His Modern Rivals*, interestingly, Carroll pokes fun at the very thing for which Eperson criticizes him. At one point Minos objects to the practice of overdefining, for surely, he says, there are some things we may be assumed to know (*EMR*, III, ii, 1, p. 185). Later he ridicules another geometrician's definition because it introduces a kind of circulating tautology. The proposed definition reads: " 'A *Theorem* is the formal statement of a Proposition that may be demonstrated from known Propositions. These known Propositions may themselves be Theorems or Axioms!' " Minos is baffled by this declaration, but in all mock seriousness proposes the following interpretation: "Perhaps . . . it is intended that the teacher who uses this Manual should, on reading the words "a Proposition that may be demonstrated,' recognize the fact that this is itself 'a Theorem,' and at once go back to the beginning of the sentence. He will thus obtain a Definition closely resembling a Continued Fraction, and may go on repeating, as long as his breath holds out, or until his pupil declares himself satisfied, 'a Theorem is the formal statement of the formal

---

[28] See Dodgson, *Euclid Books I, II With Words Substituted for the Algebraical Symbols Used in the First Edition*, 2d ed. (London, 1883); Eperson, "Lewis Carroll—Mathematician," *Mathematical Gazette*, XVII (May 1933), 92–94.

statement of the formal statement of the—!'" (*EMR*, III, ii, 1, p. 189).

For Carroll, language itself is incorrigibly tricky. He is ultracautious, for instance, in letter to the grown-up Alice, Mrs. Hargreaves: "If your husband is here he would be (most) very welcome. (I crossed out most because it is ambiguous—most words are, I fear.)"[29] Carroll recognizes the problematical nature of any attempt to define and fix once and for all the shifting muddle of possible mental universes. He does, however, gallantly so attempt. The first book of *Symbolic Logic* is devoted to the painstaking laying out of groundwork, all founded on a discussion of Things and their Attributes. A Thing is basically a substantive, an Attribute an adjective or adjective phrase or clause.

In this book Carroll does not go into the peculiar symbiosis which obtains between Things and Attributes, but he does so in the prototype of *Symbolic Logic*, that is, *The Game of Logic*. Here the question is clearly asked, but not answered: whether a Thing can exist without its Attributes or vice versa (*GL*, pp. 2–3). This is pertinent to my working model of terms and rules in a game. That is, a term is a Thing, and a rule, in one of its most obvious forms, amounts to a species of Attribute defining that Thing. A Thing is meaningful precisely in its relation to the whole universe in which it exists, virtually all of which might be specified in an elaborate Attribute for the Thing in question. As we see in *Hoyle*, chess pieces are defined in terms of their Attributes, how they move, what they can do. The same general case obtains in Carroll's rules for Court Circular, though here it is not moves that are important but values of various combinations of cards in relation to the whole system.[30]

[29] From Captain Caryl Hargreaves, "Lewis Carroll as Recalled by Alice," *New York Times* (May 1, 1932), quoted in Lennon, p. 195.

[30] *Hoyle*, pp. 207–208; Carroll (Anonymous), "Rules for Court Circular," *Works*, pp. 1265–1269.

In his *Course in General Linguistics* Ferdinand de Saussure makes an analogy between the systems of language and chess: "Just as the game of chess is entirely in the combination of the different chess pieces, language is characterized as a system based entirely on the opposition of its concrete units . . . and still, delimiting them is such a delicate problem that we may wonder at first if they really exist." For: "To consider a term as simply the union of a certain sound with a certain concept is grossly misleading. To define it this way would isolate the term from its system; it would mean assuming that one can start from the terms and construct the system by adding them together when, on the contrary, it is from the interdependent whole that one must start and through analysis obtain its elements."[31]

Carroll chooses to proceed as if delimited terms, Things, existed, as if they could be considered in isolation. This is a matter of expositional convenience for him, though as we have seen, in *The Game of Logic* he concedes the great difficulty of dissociating what is actually a dialectical unity. It is also a matter of convenience to me to use Elizabeth Sewell's definition of a game, with its notion of distinct terms and rules, even though it must be remembered that each is to be conceived in relation to the other.[32]

Piaget compares games and language and makes a point about the arbitrariness of langue systems: "Collective games are to individual symbols [found especially in the second stage

[31] De Saussure, *Course in General Linguistics*, ed. Charles Bully and Albert Sechehaye, in collaboration with Albert Reidlinger, trans. Wade Baskin (New York, 1959), pp. 107, 113.

[32] See also Hugh Kenner, "Art in a Closed Field," *Virginia Quarterly Review*, XXXVIII (Autumn 1962), 600, 599. Ratifying Sewell's position with regard to Carroll and other modern authors, Kenner says, "The closed field contains a finite number of elements [terms] to be combined according to fixed rules." He also remarks, "Put this way it sounds like a game."

of play, that of fantasy] as socialized language is to egocentric language." He explains what he means by egocentric language in *The Language and Thought of the Child*: the child younger than seven or seven and a half (Alice's ages, by the way), tends to be ego-centered in his attitude because in speaking he does not always care first and foremost about making himself understood or understanding others; he still shows a strong interest in simply establishing his own sense of control over a sound system—the ritual of articulation for the sake of the ritual. His words often have a private significance. Piaget says that this young child uses "symbols," that is, "motivated" or associational signifiers, both in his language and in his play. "Signs," in the sense conceived by the school of de Saussure, belong to older children and typify socialized language and socialized play—games with rules (Piaget's third stage). Signs are arbitrary signifiers, estabished by convention, not by inherent symbolic association. As de Saussure has it, linguistic signs (like those in his own example, chess, the rule game par excellence) are arbitrary, purely conventional, and meaningful only on the basis of phonemic contrast.[33]

Carroll makes the following point about the arbitrariness and conventionality of language: "No word has a meaning inseparably attached to it; a word means what the speaker intends by it, and what the hearer understands by it, and that is all." To illustrate de Saussure's point that minimal differentiation makes intelligibility, examples from Carroll may also be cited. In *Looking-Glass*, Chapter XII, Alice asks concerning her kitten, who does nothing but purr, " 'But how *can* you talk with a person if they *always* say the same thing?' " T. E. Hulme points out that Humpty-Dumpty's principle of identification as applied to human faces—the desirability of mini-

[33] Piaget, *Play, Dreams and Imitation*, p. 139; Piaget, *The Language and Thought of the Child*, pref. E. Claparède, trans. Marjorie and Ruth Gabain, 3d ed. (London, New York, 1959), p. 176; Piaget, *Play, Dreams and Imitation*, pp. 169–170; de Saussure, p. 68.

mally differentiated arrangement of eyes, nose, mouth—is the basis of all science and all philosophy. In *Lewis Carroll, Semeiotician* Donald Kirk remarks that not being able to tell things apart contributes to Wonderland nonsense, for whatever sense is, being able to tell one thing from another helps to make it.[34]

One of de Saussure's most interesting ideas is a kind of paradoxical corollary to the arbitrariness of the sign, the fact that it is made up by people and works between them only by agreement. Namely, because the sign is conventional it is, for all purposes of the individual, immutable. The community has created the sign by fiat, with no justification beyond its own will, but it cannot change the sign at will. In the realest sense one is dictated to by institutions as already evolved. Just so, the social, reciprocal, necessarily rule-bound nature of game institutions gives them a solid existence persistent through time and in the face of the caprice, the idiosyncrasies, even the rebelliousness of players. The "particular sense of freedom" that Sewell finds within the game sphere exists, but it is the specially qualified "freedom" of law and inevitably implies restriction, compulsion, limitation. This can very easily be felt as impingement upon personal liberty. Consider Carroll's remark in "Twelve Months in a Curatorship by One Who Has Tried It" (1884) concerning a new code of rules which fitted him to a T, like a new pair of handcuffs.[35]

[34] Carroll, "The Stage and the Spirit of Reverence," from *The Theatre* (June 1888), rprt. in Collingwood, ed., *Diversions and Digressions*, p. 183; Carroll, *Through the Looking-Glass and What Alice Found There*, in *The Annotated Alice*, ed. Gardner, p. 241; Hulme, "Cinders," p. 222; Kirk, *Lewis Carroll, Semeiotician*, University of Florida Monographs, Humanities, No. 11 (Fall 1962), (Gainsville, Florida, 1963), pp. 66–67. For another linguistic study of Carroll (including a brief section on language as play) see Robert Donald Sutherland, *Language and Lewis Carroll*, No. 26; *Janua Linguarum Studia Memoriae Nicolai Van Wijk Dedicata*, ed. C. H. Van Schooneveld (Mouton, 1970).

[35] Carroll (Anonymous), "Twelve Months in a Curatorship by One Who Has Tried It," *Works*, p. 1180.

For a pleasant description of the way that the game of language can most maddeningly master and defeat the unfortunate player if he does not take the considerable trouble to get the upper hand himself, let us look at Carroll's *Wonderland Postage-Stamp Case and Eight or Nine Wise Words about Letter-Writing* (1890). We see here that if we are going to play the game at all, what is needed to prevent conventions from getting the better of us is more rules, not fewer (and certainly not no rules), so as to render those conventions controllable, reliable, manipulatable, in a word, certain. This achieved, we may if we like employ the system to get the better of somebody else, as provided for, for example, in Carroll's Ciphers.

The Game of Communication

"In the Game of Whist, Hoyle gives us one golden Rule, 'When in doubt, win the trick'—I find that Rule admirable for real life: when in doubt what to do, I 'make-up' my Letter-Register!" (*Works*, p. 1225).[36]

In his *Wonderland Postage-Stamp Case and Eight or Nine Wise Words about Letter-Writing* Carroll gives many golden rules. Most tell us how, with incredible labor, foresight, organization, caution, and perseverance, to achieve accuracy of communication in the teeth of overwhelming odds.

The *Wonderland Postage-Stamp Case*, in which *Eight or Nine Wise Words* is tidily packaged, itself perhaps illustrates the confusing tendency of one thing to turn into another when one least expects it. In colored versions of Tenniel's drawings, Alice nurses the Duchess's baby on the front, the Cheshire Cat grins on the back. Pull out the inner envelope, however, and the baby is a pig, the Cheshire Cat a mere ghost of him-

[36] See Carroll, *The Wonderland Postage-Stamp Case and Eight or Nine Wise Words about Letter-Writing* (Oxford, 1890), for the ingenious "Pictorial Surprises." For convenience I refer in the text to this piece in *Works*, pp. 1211–1225.

self. These "Pictorial Surprises" are amusing, but as Carroll points out in the course of his *Wise Words*, some of the surprises to be encountered in letters written without benefit of careful rules can cause serious dismay, dismay greater even than Alice's in the presence (and absence) of the transforming baby and cat. This little treatise is all about pinning things down—in this case language—so they can't get away or suddenly change into something else.

One must be able to recognize and be certain of a thing; for example, the true Wonderland Postage-Stamp Case may be certainly recognized because it is one of a class: "Some American writer has said 'the snakes in this district may be divided into one species—the venomous.' The same principle applies here. Postage-Stamp-Cases may be divided into one species— the 'Wonderland!' Imitations of it may soon appear, no doubt: but they cannot include the two Pictorial Surprises, which are copyright" (*Works*, p. 1211). It is harder to get a copyright on your words and meaning in a letter so as to be able to trade back and forth with confidence, but this is what Carroll proposes to help us do.

Almost without exception Carroll's rules are predicated upon a general assumption: whatever miscarriages of communication can happen, will. The first set of instructions on "How To Begin a Letter" thus tells us to get out the correspondent's last letter and reread it for his present address, never trusting for a moment to treacherous memory. "Otherwise," Carroll assures us, it must follow as the night the day that "you will be sending your letter to his regular address in *London*, though he has been careful in writing to give you his *Torquay* address in full" (*Works*, pp. 1212–1213).

Care on his part will go for nothing without complementary care on yours. You must give your address and the date in full (only hoping that he will play according to the same rule-book). Nothing, or as little as possible is to be assumed. For instance, a cryptic address like "Dover" will not do the trick;

one cannot leave the details to be culled from a previous letter, as that has undoubtedly been destroyed.

Mere knowledge of information—the full and correct address in this instance—is not enough. One must also transfer this knowledge without impairment to paper, and then empower it for the physical transfer to another's hands, let alone his understanding. What this means practically is legible addressing and the appropriate stamp, both to be taken care of before it is even worthwhile to begin the letter proper. " 'What! Before writing the Letter?' Most certainly. And I'll tell you what will happen if you don't. You will go on writing till the last moment, and, just in the middle of the last sentence, you will become aware that 'time's up!' Then come the hurried wind-up—the wildly-scrawled signature—the hastily fastened envelope, which comes open in the post—the address, a mere hieroglyphic—the horrible discovery that you've forgotten to replenish your Stamp-Case, . . ." and so on, with wild appeals for stamps, arrival at the post office, too late, and the upshot, "return of the Letter, from the Dead-Letter Office, marked 'address illegible!' " (*Works*, p. 1213).

Legibility is also the golden rule of the next section, "How to Go on with a Letter." Carroll tells the story of a scrawl he once received in the mail which he used to carry about with him in his pocket, looking at it in odd moments. Isolated words would reveal themselves by flashes, and these fixed, context would help with the others. But if the context should fail? For example, foreign names of people and places are impossible to decipher; they give one no grounds even for an intelligent guess.

The advice that follows in this section concerns insuring oneself against charges of misinterpretation of the letter to which one is responding. Again, don't trust memory or the other's faith in one's memory. Write with his letter open before you. And in referring to anything he has said, prudence dictates, *"quote the exact words"*; never rely on paraphrase.

Carroll expresses extreme suspicion of the accuracy and reliability of language as it issues from two different mouths or pens: "A's impression, of what B has said, expressed in A's words, will never convey to B the meaning of his own words" (*Works*, p. 1215). And precautions must be doubled in the case of a controversy, which wedges people's meanings further than ever apart. Besides being careful to quote your correspondent's words exactly, you must guard yourself by keeping a copy of your own words. Then if need be in the course of the altercation, you may deny with confidence his misrepresentation of your statements.

It is not only another who may misrepresent your meaning; it is also yourself, particularly when you risk a dangerous figure of speech, an exaggeration, or jest, which proceeds by indirection. Carroll's "Seventh Rule" is one especially applicable to himself, one which he did not always apply with adequate force, considering misunderstandings that arose in more than one of his correspondences with child-friends. The rule reads: "If it should ever occur to you to write, jestingly, in *dispraise* of your friend, be sure you exaggerate enough to make the jesting *obvious*: a word spoken in jest, but taken as earnest, may lead to very serious consequences" (*Works*, p. 1216).

Of first importance is that the play arena be staked out and recognized as such by all players, and not mistaken for an earnest workplace. Considering that where communication is concerned, nothing is obvious for Carroll (hence the elaborate rules), to make one's playful attitude obvious takes some ingenuity. He was compelled, for example, to write an apology to Ella Monier-Williams for a hoax that he had carried very far; he had convinced her by means of clever equivocations that her journal was actually to be published in *The Monthly Packet*, a joke that she had unfortunately been tricked into swallowing.[37]

[37] See Carroll, *Letters*, pp. 87–89. Ella Monier-Williams was hoaxed into

Carroll cautions us against trusting words for a minute: to prevent a thing from becoming a lie, willy-nilly, as you say it, actually do it. For example, when you say you are enclosing a check, leave off writing, go and get the check, and enclose it. As an illustration perhaps of how insidious untruthfulness can be, Carroll gives us an "old" proverb forbidding cross writing: *"Cross writing makes cross reading."* It turns out that that this saying isn't so old after all; "In fact," Carroll admits three sentences later, "I'm afraid I invented it while writing this paragraph!" Lies and misrepresentations are like automatic writing: they come of themselves. Besides, truth is relative, and so is the word "old," which Carroll tells us by way of sophistical explanation for his invention, "is a *comparative* term." It is true in a sense that the proverb, being written in the paragraph, is more "old" than it might be if it hadn't been written (*Works,* p. 1217).

The next step is "How to End a Letter." We have already been warned against the illusion of finality in any transaction of words and thoughts between people: *"Don't try to have the last word!"* It is impossible anyhow; what usually happens

---

believing that her journal was actually to be published. Carroll wrote to her during the winter of 1873, "I . . . hope you will not be annoyed at my sending three short chapters of extracts from it, to be published in *The Monthly Packet,"* and later that "every word of my letter was strictly true" and also that "Miss Yonge *has not declined* the MS." Once Ella was thoroughly taken in and had written expressing her pleasure, Carroll finally responded, "My Dear Ella, I'm afraid I have hoaxed you too much. But it really was true. I 'hoped you wouldn't be too annoyed at my &c.,' for the very good reason that I hadn't done it. . . . Miss Younge hasn't declined it—because she hasn't seen it," and so on. This letter reveals Carroll's own application of his rule for exact quoting of ambiguous words, of which he obviously kept a record. More questionable is whether or not he followed his rule for making obvious the distinction between jest and earnest. As Florence Becker Lennon remarks (p. 212), he graded his style according to the ages of his child-friends, and expected children over ten to understand his jokes and not be hurt by his teasing. But he did not always succeed in estimating the level at which he would be interpreted.

is that a controversy does not reach a conclusion but repeats itself: "To repeat your arguments, all over again, will simply lead to his doing the same; and so you will go on, like a Circulating Decimal. Did you ever know a Circulating Decimal to come to an end?" (*Works*, pp. 1216, 1215).

Just as every game needs a stop rule to prevent its going on indefinitely, so does a letter. Moves of the end game include "yours faithfully," "yours truly," "yours most truly," or "yours affectionately," depending on the tone and intimacy of the correspondent's last letter. The rule is that our wind-up should be *"at least as friendly as his,"* maybe a trace more friendly. The final move is the Postscript, which too carries a message, depending on the correspondent. For instance, if his last is an apology for some negligence, forgiveness comes in the most friendly form in a P.S. It serves to throw the matter into the shade as something so little worthy a fuss, it comes as an afterthought (*Works*, pp. 1217–1218).

All these rules may be followed, yet letters miscarry unless transported to the post by hand. Put them in your pocket, or, Carroll's experience dictates most fatally, "you will take a long country-walk . . . , passing the Post-Office *twice*, going and returning, and when you get home, will find them *still* in your pocket" (*Works*, p. 1218).

The last section of *Eight or Nine Wise Words*, "On Registering Correspondence," presents a beautifully elaborate system of recording all letters received or sent, complete with an intermesh of numbers, symbols, multicolored lines, and a prescribed spatial arrangement (that is, write on the righthand side of the ledger book; at the bottom of each page turn the book upside down and head down the right side again). A précis of each letter is included to bolster fainting memory (so little to be counted on, as we have seen). It establishes a thing consoling to contemplate in times to come—chronological order. It secures that letters will eventually be answered, which, bearing in mind Carroll's basic assumption that what can go wrong, will, we must recognize as the first security to establish in letter writing, without which all the others go for nothing.

Filling-in, cross-referencing, head- and footnoting, and triumphant crossing-off constitute "making-up" the entry book, and this is to be done in "odd moments of leisure." Making-up, though it looks complicated (and it certainly does), is recommended "as a pleasant occupation for a rainy day, or at any time that you feel disinclined for more severe mental work" (*Works*, pp. 1223, 1225). The line between work and game is dim here. The letter register is to be undertaken because it is pleasant to do; insofar as it is also useful, it is so because it helps one succeed in the game of communication. Remember, *Eight or Nine Wise Words* is the *Hoyle* of letter writing.[38]

The idea behind *Eight or Nine Wise Words* is that every stratagem must be used to ensure, against tremendous odds, the understanding of the reader, however ordinary his interpretive ability. In Carroll's two message ciphers, the Telegraph-Cipher and Alphabet-Cipher of 1868, the reverse is the case. Here the idea is by ingenious strategies to prevent understanding by the ordinary reader, to enable the message to be deciphered only by him who is in on the rules. These rules might be compared to the signal code agreed upon by the partners in a game such as bridge. Partners aim to communicate one with the other, but to retain secrecy before the wily opponent.

The Telegraph-Cipher has not been reprinted, but according to Roger Lancelyn Green, on the whole it resembles the Alphabet-Cipher.[39] The latter involves a "dictionary of symbols"— letters representing the alphabet as in Figure 1.

[38] See also "Preface," *Sylvie and Bruno Concluded*, pp. x–xi, where Carroll insists on spelling and punctuating according to rule; later he mentions a "Code of Rules for Letter-Writing" as an invention sure to make one famous (pp. 116–117).

[39] The Telegraph-Cipher was invented in 1868, as mentioned in the *Diaries*, April 22, 1868, II, 268–269. It was never reprinted but resembles

	A	B	**C**	D	**E**	F	**G**	H	**I**	J	K	**L**	M	**N**	O	P	Q	R	S	T	U	**V**	W	X	Y	Z	
A	a	b	c	d	e	f	g	h	i	j	k	l	m	n	o	p	q	r	s	t	u	v	w	x	y	z	A
B	b	c	d	e	f	g	h	i	j	k	l	m	n	o	p	q	r	s	t	u	v	w	x	y	z	a	B
C	c	d	e	f	g	h	i	j	k	l	m	n	o	p	q	r	s	t	u	v	w	x	y	z	a	b	C
D	d	e	f	g	h	i	j	k	l	m	n	o	p	q	r	s	t	u	v	w	x	y	z	a	b	c	D
E	e	f	g	h	i	j	k	l	m	n	o	p	q	r	s	t	u	v	w	x	y	z	a	b	c	d	E
F	f	g	h	i	j	k	l	m	n	o	p	q	r	s	t	u	v	w	x	y	z	a	b	c	d	e	F
G	g	h	i	j	k	l	m	n	o	p	q	r	s	t	u	v	w	x	y	z	a	b	c	d	e	f	G
H	h	i	j	k	l	m	n	o	p	q	r	s	t	u	v	w	x	y	z	a	b	c	d	e	f	g	H
I	i	j	k	l	m	n	o	p	q	r	s	t	u	v	w	x	y	z	a	b	c	d	e	f	g	h	I
J	j	k	l	m	n	o	p	q	r	s	t	u	v	w	x	y	z	a	b	c	d	e	f	g	h	i	J
K	k	l	m	n	o	p	q	r	s	t	u	v	w	x	y	z	a	b	c	d	e	f	g	h	i	j	K
L	l	m	n	o	p	q	r	s	t	u	v	w	x	y	z	a	b	c	d	e	f	g	h	i	j	k	L
M	m	n	o	p	q	r	s	t	u	v	w	x	y	z	a	b	c	d	e	f	g	h	i	j	k	l	M
N	n	o	p	q	r	s	t	u	v	w	x	y	z	a	b	c	d	e	f	g	h	i	j	k	l	m	N
O	o	p	q	r	s	t	u	v	w	x	y	z	a	b	c	d	e	f	g	h	i	j	k	l	m	n	O
P	p	q	r	s	t	u	v	w	x	y	z	a	b	c	d	e	f	g	h	i	j	k	l	m	n	o	P
Q	q	r	s	t	u	v	w	x	y	z	a	b	c	d	e	f	g	h	i	j	k	l	m	n	o	p	Q
R	r	s	t	u	v	w	x	y	z	a	b	c	d	e	f	g	h	i	j	k	l	m	n	o	p	q	R
S	s	t	u	v	w	x	y	z	a	b	c	d	e	f	g	h	i	j	k	l	m	n	o	p	q	r	S
T	t	u	v	w	x	y	z	a	b	c	d	e	f	g	h	i	j	k	l	m	n	o	p	q	r	s	T
U	u	v	w	x	y	z	a	b	c	d	e	f	g	h	i	j	k	l	m	n	o	p	q	r	s	t	U
V	v	w	x	y	z	a	b	c	d	e	f	g	h	i	j	k	l	m	n	o	p	q	r	s	t	u	V
W	w	x	y	z	a	b	c	d	e	f	g	h	i	j	k	l	m	n	o	p	q	r	s	t	u	v	W
X	x	y	z	a	b	c	d	e	f	g	h	i	j	k	l	m	n	o	p	q	r	s	t	u	v	w	X
Y	y	z	a	b	c	d	e	f	g	h	i	j	k	l	m	n	o	p	q	r	s	t	u	v	w	x	Y
Z	z	a	b	c	d	e	f	g	h	i	j	k	l	m	n	o	p	q	r	s	t	u	v	w	x	y	Z
	A	B	**C**	D	**E**	F	**G**	H	**I**	J	K	**L**	M	**N**	O	P	Q	R	S	T	U	**V**	W	X	Y	Z	

Figure 1. Lewis Carroll's Alphabet-Cipher, printed anonymously on an undated card. (I have circled the letters of the key-word.)

Two correspondents share a key-word or sentence. The letters constituting the key-word—here, v i g i l a n c e—are circled along the top and bottom of the chart. When the correspondents wish to communicate, they write this key-word over the message. It indicates which column is to be used to translate each letter of the message into code (*Works*, pp. 1283–1284).[40]

Here is the illustration Carroll uses to explain the system.

To Code:

(key-word)   v i g i l a n c e v i g i l a n c e v i g i l a n c e v i

(message)   m e e t m e o n t u e s d a y e v e n i n g a t s e v e n

(cipher)   h m k b x e b p x p m y l l y r x i i q t o l t f g z z v

Then to decode:

(key-word)   v i g i l a n c e v i g i l a n c e v i g i l a n c e v i

(cipher)   h m k b x e b p x p m y l l y r x i i q t o l t f g z z v

(message)   m e e t m e o n t u e s d a y e v e n i n g a t s e v e n

Carroll also explains the procedure in a letter to Edith Argyles, where, amusingly, the key-word is "trick."[41] That is what the cipher is basically. And indeed, "vigilance," the key-word in our example above, is another basic, for the cipher operates on the assumption of the ever-presence of the very cleverest of cipher-breakers, who, given the slightest opportunity, will break the system and divine the message. Hence the direction to destroy the paper on which the message has

---

the Alphabet-Cipher, according to Roger Lancelyn Green's note. Though the Alphabet-Cipher is not mentioned in the diary, it is also probably from 1868, according to Williams and Madan (p. 44). However, the letters to the Argyles children of April 22 and April 29, 1868, *Letters*, pp. 50, 52–53, clearly refer to the Alphabet-Cipher, which then must have been invented at least by this date.

[40] Carroll (Anonymous), "The Alphabet-Cipher," *Works*, pp. 1283–1284; page references in the text.

[41] Carroll, *Letters*, April 29, 1868, pp. 52–53.

been encoded beneath the guiding key-word. Hence also the careful warning: although it would be absolutely necessary to keep a dictionary of symbols including only those columns dictated by the key-word, this would be unwise, as the abbreviated dictionary is liable to be found by alien decipherers. Therefore only the complete table should be retained. This will assure a triumph of selective unintelligibility, quite opposite from that striven after by the follower of *Eight or Nine Wise Words*: "It will now be impossible for anyone, ignorant of the key-word, to decipher the message, even with the help of the table" (*Works*, p. 1284).

As in other secret language games that children delight in, the use of the cipher is not practical but purely psychological; it gives one a charming sense of mastery or superiority over those who can't understand it and are made miserable by that fact. Carroll's letter on the Alphabet-Cipher to Dolly Argyles makes this appeal clear: "Don't let Edith torture you with that funny way of writing, but tell her I'm going to send her a better way that'll make her hair stand on end with delight. Babies of six months old easily learn how to write it in a minute, and a whole regiment with fixed bayonets couldn't find it out in a fortnight without knowing the key-word."[42] The pleasure derived from letter writing issues mainly from mastering a very unruly system, but with the ciphers one may enjoy a mastery headier still—over a living opponent.

Game Theory and Carroll: Rational Players, Choice of Universe, Infinity, and How to Stop Once Started?

The modern theory of games mathematically describes the structure of conflicts between opposing interests, conflicts that appear at their simplest and most formalized in parlor games.

[42] Carroll, *Letters*, April 22, 1868, p. 50.

Because play in Carroll's writing characteristically assumes the agonistic form of games with rules, the general ideas of game theory may help us understand Carroll, understand especially the games that Alice comes up against.

An essential and problematical postulate of game theory is that calling for "rational players." Anatol Rapoport defines a rational player as one who is able to choose consistently among all possible risky outcomes, according to what he calls "utility theory." A rational player is assumed to be fully cognizant of the terms and rules of the game and of the utilities (the pattern of consistent preferences among possible payoffs) of the other players, an assumption open to question in the case of Alice, as we shall see in the next chapters. In addition, it is assumed that a player faced with two alternatives will choose the one yielding the preferred outcome; in other words, he will always maximize utility, a choice notably unavailable to Alice most of the time because of the failure of the first assumption.[43]

Rapoport describes the peculiar limitations involved in assumptions about rationality. One paradox of rationality is revealed in the analysis of what are called nonzero-sum, nonnegotiable games. These differ from the simple, zero-sum, parlor type, which are all-or-nothing, win-or-lose in outcome. Nonzero-sum games, as the term implies, provide for possible solutions which could be agreed upon as desirable for both parties. But they are nonnegotiable according to the simple standards of rationality we are familiar with from zero-sum conflicts. An example of such a game might be the nuclear conflict game. But as Rapoport demonstrates, in such a conflict, "if each player assumes that the other is individually rational, both can rationalize a strategy which is not collectively ra-

---

[43] Rapoport, pp. 34, 200–201; see also R. Duncan Luce and Howard Raiffa, *Games and Decisions* (New York, London, Sydney, 1957), pp. 47–50.

tional." (We of the age of nuclear-powered political "game plans" all know what this means, without mathematics.) Rapoport concludes that game theory has so far been operating upon a single narrow criterion of rationality which leads it to a dead end, because "the sine qua non of game theory [and of the typical game player's attitude] is that it can get started only after the utilities are given. It never questions the rationality of the goals pursued by the contending powers."[44]

Carroll does not deal with nonzero-sum, nonnegotiable games as such, but he does deal with the general issue they raise: the possibility that the player may be acting rationally and yet the system in which he operates remain utterly crazy in relation to some larger context. The rationality of the interior disables the player's ability to reason from a standpoint outside the game. It is a rationality which has nothing to say about choice of universe. Alice, for example, is confronted by discrete mental systems or games, among which she may choose. The problem is simply choosing.

Rapoport makes another point about rationality: "The fundamental assumption of game theory [and game players] is that everything there is to know about a situation is known at the start by 'rational players,' and 'stays put' as they reason about the situation. Reflexive reasoning, on the other hand, 'folds in on itself,' as it were and so is not a finite process."[45] What happens when one begins to reason about the rationale of the rules of the game?

Carroll, as well as Rapoport, was intrigued by the problem of infinite regression. This problem, which has regularly pestered logic, results from the necessity for but the great difficulty of obtaining finitude in the closed-set reasoning that typifies the rationality of the game player and indeed most rational thought as we have been accustomed to think of it. Bertrand Russell found that the most logically difficult and important (as opposed to merely agreeable) of Carroll's mathe-

44 Rapoport, pp. 143, 213.
45 Rapoport, p. 143.

matical achievements consists of two puzzles submitted to
Mind in 1894. Both puzzles concern Hypotheticals. The second is the more interesting because it neatly illustrates a potential fatality in traditional sequential logic: the reasoner
finds himself laboring upon an infinitely unfolding ladder of
enabling rungs, each of which then logically demands its own
endless series of enablers.

The piece, called "What the Tortoise Said to Achilles,"[46]
takes up Achilles as he has overtaken the Tortoise in the
famous old race (reputedly first suggested by Zeno) of which
it was said the thing couldn't be done. Achilles crows that he
has done it, but the sagacious, ever-patient Tortoise knows
better. He entices Achilles to embark upon a different, mental
racecourse, also consisting of an infinite number of distances,
but in this case each longer than the one before. Of course,
our hero can't win either way.

As Achilles sits upon the Tortoise's back, notebook (conveniently plentiful in blank pages) in hand, the Tortoise cites
an example of a segment of argument from Euclid's First
Proposition. This consists of two steps and a conclusion:

(A) Things that are equal to the same are equal to each
other.

(B) The two sides of this Triangle are things that are
equal to the same.

(Z) The two sides of this Triangle are equal to each other.

The reader might exist, the Tortoise declares, who accepted
A and *B* as true but not the Hypothetical *Z*. The problem
posed to Achilles is, assuming the Tortoise to be such a reader,
to force him logically to accept *Z* as true. As it turns out, to
Achilles' grief, the only way to do this is to keep adding pro-
visional Hypotheticals, that is: "(C) If *A* and *B* are true, *Z*

[46] Bertrand Russell, in Mark Van Doren, ed., "Lewis Carroll, *Alice in
Wonderland*," in *The New Invitation to Learning*, pp. 214–218; Carroll
(Anonymous), "What the Tortoise Said to Achilles," from *Mind* (1894),
Works, pp. 1225–1230; page references in the text.

must be true"; "(D) If A and B and C are true, Z must be true"; "(E) If A and B and C and D are true, Z must be true"; and so on. Each step is longer than the one before. Gradually it dawns on the unfortunate Achilles that there will be no end to this race. When last seen by the narrator of the incident, he is writing down Hypothetical one thousand and one and exhibiting the classic signs of despair.

"What the Tortoise Said to Achilles" illustrates the liability of the "accepted facts of logic" to infinite regression, once pushed. Euclid wouldn't have progressed beyond his First Proposition had he been as relentlessly logical as the Tortoise. Achilles says, after he has tried A, B, C, and D on the Tortoise, that logic will "force" the Tortoise to accept Z. "Whatever *Logic* is good enough to tell me," replies the Tortoise, "is worth *writing* down" (*Works*, p. 1229). Thus may we become involved in a spiraling series of metalanguages (or metalogics or metamathematics), each acting as the proviso that stands outside and enables the next.

A similar situation has been discussed in relation to the White Knight's song in *Alice through the Looking-Glass*. Ernest Nagel points out in "Symbolic Notation, Haddocks' Eyes, and the Dog-Walking Ordinance" that this song, as introduced by the White Knight, involves names of names, labels of labels, language used to describe language. Alice insists on confusing the various metalanguages applied to the song, while the White Knight knows that these exist on entirely different planes of reference and must be kept separate. Here is Nagel's chart:

The call-name of the name of	
The Song	= "Haddocks' Eyes"
The name of The Song	= "The Aged Aged Man"
The call-name of The Song	= "Ways and Means"
The Song	= A-sitting on a Gate[47]

Roger Holmes insists in "The Philosopher's Alice in Won-

[47] Nagel, "Symbolic Notation, Haddocks' Eyes, and the Dog-Walking

derland" that the song should equal the actual singing of it. But this overlooks the fact that just as in the case of "What the Tortoise Said to Achilles," metalanguages are capable of infinite extension, and it would be quite possible for the White Knight to go on saying what the song is (compare Achilles' endless "writing down") without ever getting to the singing at all. That he does so is a sort of leap, like that which the Euclidian reasoner makes, be it sooner or later, to the final Z.[48]

As the logician Ralph Monroe Eaton says, "an act of violence (i.e., judgment, belief) [remember Carroll's advice to a child-friend not to wear out her powers of pure willful acts of belief] is necessary to break a chain of *implications* and effect the passage to an *inference*." A cut is needed in the chain of Hypotheticals or metalinguistic propositions. Otherwise infinity threatens to engulf us, and we will get nowhere at all.[49]

Carroll clearly feels the presence of such infinities in one form or another, and though he is certainly able to joke on the subject, he prefers comfortable finitude wherever he can get it. For example, in *Euclid and His Modern Rivals* Minos remarks that, confronted with the words *"every* cubic inch of Space,"* his mind is unable to deal with the matter at all. He contends that it would be less unnerving to phrase the same concept as *"any* cubic inch (*EMR*, I, ii, 4. p. 25).

Ordinance," in *The World of Mathematics*, ed. James R. Newman, 4 vols. (London, 1956), II, 1889; see also J. F. Thomson, "What Achilles Should Have Said to the Tortoise," *Ratio*, III (1960), 95–105. To escape his difficulty, Thomson argues, Achilles should have refused to fall into the infinite-regress trap; logicians recognize that to include a proviso about the validity of their logic as a premise in a specific argument mixes two levels of thought and infinitely expands reasoning by making it reasoning about reasoning; it must be disallowed if the train of thought is to arrive anywhere.

[48] Holmes, "The Philosopher's Alice in Wonderland," *Antioch Review*, XIX (Summer 1959), 138–139.

[49] Eaton, *General Logic: An Introductory Survey* (New York, 1931), p. 43.

The incident between Achilles and the Tortoise takes place in the context of a game; it is presented as a version of a race in logical terms. Now one of the features of a game is that its terms and rules stand on no more solid a basis of "because" than Euclid's rule that if A and B are true, Z is true. And just as the game has its beginning by arbitrary fiat, so does it have its ending. One rule which is absolutely necessary is a stop rule. Writers on game theory tell us that all parlor games are so provided.[50]

The originator of modern game theory, John Von Neumann, states that the rules of the game must at some point stop the procedure. "Now this *stop rule* must be such as to give a certainty that every conceivable play will be stopped sometime." For some games, like most kinds of cards, this is relatively easy to provide for. Interestingly though, it is not so simple for chess, which in some situations may threaten to go on and on without a clear conclusion. Hence the various elaborate tie rules for the end game of chess. One is a sort of "rule of three" that says that any cycle of choices (or moves), when three times repeated, terminates the play by a tie. But this fails to provide for all possible cases (where, for example, repetitious moves might be avoided) and is therefore not a thoroughly effective stop rule. Another stop rule says that if no pawn is moved or officer taken for forty moves, a tie ensues. Chess notoriously can fail of a simple, quick, humane ending. Forty moves is a long time to wait for legal execution. And why not thirty-nine or forty-one?[51]

[50] Rapoport, p. 20; Luce and Raiffa, p. 41.

[51] John Von Neumann and Oskar Morgenstern, *Theory of Games and Economic Behavior*, 3d ed. (New York, London, Sydney, 1944), pp. 59–60 and nn. 3, 4. According to Von Neumann: "The obvious way to guarantee this [an end] is to devise a stop rule for which it is certain that the stop will come before a fixed moment, say v^*. I.e. that while v [length of the game] may depend on $\sigma_1, \sigma_2, \sigma_3, \ldots$ [the succession of moves], it is to be $v \leqq v^*$ where v^* does not depend on $\sigma_1, \sigma_2, \sigma_3, \ldots$. If this is the case we say that the stop rule is *bounded by* v^*." Chess, it turns out, is

The problematical nature of the stop rule in chess, a rule essential to the achievement of finitude necessary to any game, casts into sharp relief the arbitrariness of this rule. For as I interpret Von Neumann's analysis, the end of a game is like a brick wall erected at the end of a universe; in chess especially one may well wonder not only what lies on the other side, but couldn't it just as well have been placed one step, in this case one move, further off? Game theory helps to reveal the literally artificial nature of our mental universes, an artificiality of which Carroll was very much aware, and which he often presents by means of the analogy of the game.

---

hard to stop without an enormous v^*. Thus: "From a purely mathematical point of view, the following question could be asked: Let the stop rule be effective in this sense only, that it is impossible so to arrange the successive choices $\sigma_1, \sigma_2, \sigma_3, \ldots$ that the stop never comes. I.e. let there always be a finite v dependent upon $\sigma_1, \sigma_2, \sigma_3, \ldots$. Does this by itself secure the existence of a fixed, finite v^* bounding the stop rule? I.e. such that all $v \leqq v^*$?"

3. Two Introductions
to the *Alices*

Carroll versus Wordsworth in
the White Knight's Song

From all her strange adventures, Alice remembers most clearly the White Knight's song. The Knight says this ditty is long, beautiful, and melancholy, and always brings tears to his hearers' eyes, or else it doesn't. In Alice's case it doesn't. Why should it, any more than, within the song, the aged man's wisdom should bring retrospective tears to the eyes of his interlocutor? The Knight is nearer right when he says his singing can bring Alice comfort. Unsure as he may be of the effects of his song, one way to understand it, surely, is as a whimsical taking in vain of the forms of melancholy which it recasts. What does the aged man reveal that he should be so memorable?

Alice is quite right that the Knight's song is not strictly speaking "his own invention." But though his first line resembles one from a lyric by Thomas Moore, it is not from Moore but from Wordsworth that the Knight draws his main inspiration.[1] One candidate for the target of the White Knight's

---

[1] All references to the White Knight's song are to Carroll, *Through the Looking-Glass and What Alice Found There*, in *The Annotated Alice*, ed. Gardner, pp. 307, 311–313. The novel is hereafter identified as *L-G*. I have numbered the lines of the poem for reference in the text. Alice

parody is Wordsworth's "The Thorn."[2] Several of this poem's lines, especially before revision, do sound worthy, or unworthy, enough for the Knight. For example, the White Knight's opening line, " 'I'll tell thee everything I can,' " seems to recall:

"No more I know, I wish I did,
And I would tell it all to you." [ll. 144–145]

Carroll commits blandness of the type Wordsworth sometimes allowed himself to risk. "The Thorn" exhibits what Coleridge criticizes as Wordsworth's "matter of factness,"[3] for instance, his solicitude to inform us of the precise measurements of the lamented lost baby's grave—two feet by three feet. Of course, the White Knight's song includes matters of fact that would be completely devastating to Wordsworth's sort of poetry, the very mention, say, of Rowland's Macassar-Oil.

The subject of "The Thorn," however, is not comparable with that of the White Knight's song. For such a comparison we must look to Wordsworth's "Resolution and Independence,"[4] with its theme of endurance in work and duty. This

<hr>

recognizes the original of the song to be Thomas Moore's "I give thee all, I can no more" (or "My Heart and Lute"), a lyric about the efficacy of such useless activities as love and music to "keep Life's clouds away" (*£-G*, pp. 307, and n. 9, pp. 307–311).

[2] For Wordsworth's poems "The Thorn" and "Resolution and Independence," see *The Poetical Works of William Wordsworth*, ed. from the Ms. with textual and critical notes by E. de Selincourt, 5 vols., 2d ed. (Oxford, 1952), II, 240–248, 235–240. All line references are to this edition and are given in the text. Martin Gardner sees the White Knight's song as a burlesque of "The Thorn" (*£-G*, n. 9, pp. 310–311).

[3] Samuel Taylor Coleridge, Chapter XXII, *Biographia Literaria, With His Aesthetical Letters*, ed. J. Shawcross, 2 vols. (London, 1907; rprt. 1965), II, 101.

[4] Judge Edward Abbot Parry locates the obvious parody of "Resolution and Independence" largely in the unnecessary length with which the old

is the theme that Carroll parodies, so that quite a contrary set of values comes out on top. Of course, Carroll exaggerates and even misreads Wordsworth in the interest of transforming his message into one that contributes to the theme of play in the novel.

Both "Resolution and Independence" and the White Knight's song are investigations of the question, how should one live?—posed in each case by the speculatively inclined narrator. Both the Leech-gatherer and the aged aged man answer: persevere in working. But if the answer comes from a sly old codger rather than from a revered moorland stoic, it makes a big difference in how seriously we are being invited to take the message.

The repetition with variation of a set of lines in each poem indicates a clear connection between the two. The narrative "I" of Wordsworth's poem (I will call him Wordsworth for convenience) inquires of the old Leech-gatherer he has met one summer morning on the moor, " 'How is it that you live, and what is it you do?' " (l. 88). He wants to know, " 'What occupation do you there pursue?' " (l. 119). Carroll's narrative "I" (the White Knight, whose character suits him to be the singer, although the song was actually written before *Looking-Glass*, in 1856)[5] inquires of the aged aged man he has met one summer evening a-sitting on a gate:

---

man explains what he does; see "The Early Writings of Lewis Carroll," *Cornhill Magazine*, LVI (April 1924), 459–462. In "On Lewis Carroll's Alice and Her White Knight and Wordsworth's Ode on Immortality," Horace Gregory comments on the relation of the *Alices* in general and the White Knight's song in particular to Wordsworth's poetry. His commentary is impressionistic, rather than concerned with specific texts. Mainly he claims that Alice is a "practical young female" not interested in Wordsworth's tragic view of life, as most famously represented by the "Ode" and "Resolution and Independence." Hence the taking of Wordsworth in vain in the White Knight's song; see *The Shield of Achilles: Essays on Beliefs in Poetry* (Folcroft, Pa., 1944; rprt. 1969), pp. 90–105.

[5] The 1856 version, "Upon the Lonely Moor," from *The Train: A First-*

"Who are you, aged man? . . .
And how is it you live?"

And again,

"Come, tell me how you live! . . .
And what it is you do!"   [ll. 5–6, 23, 40]

The ending of Carroll's poem likewise links it to Wordsworth's. In the original version this is especially evident. Says the White Knight:

"I think of that strange wanderer
Upon the lonely moor."   [ll. 71–72]

Says Wordsworth, " 'I'll think of the Leech-gatherer on the lonely moor!' " (l. 140). In the version sung in *Through the Looking-Glass* mention of the moor has vanished, as also the word "wanderer," which strongly associated the aged aged man with the Leech-gatherer. Still, the later ending is essentially an expansion of the original: certain misfortunes cause the White Knight not merely to think of the strange old man, but to weep at the memory.

Carroll's poem offers, in the present tense, that reminiscence which the narrator of Wordsworth's poem foresees will occur in the future. What ineffable thoughts Wordsworth is implying he will think and what circumstances might bring them on are not easy to imagine in any specific form. Carroll exaggerates the vague and non sequitur nature of these thoughts.

If the Leech-gatherer is a "something given" (l. 51), it is hard to say exactly what; whatever it is doesn't seem to amount to much. This is because the Leech-gatherer is, and many say it, a distressingly minimal character (a "stone," a "thing endued with sense," a "man not all alive nor dead")

Class Magazine, II (Oct. 1856), 255–256, appears in *The Annotated Alice*, ed. Gardner, n. 9, pp. 307–308.

(ll. 57, 61, 64).[6] Thus Carroll's opening is all too applicable to the substance of an experience such as Wordsworth's:

"I'll tell thee everything I can:
There's little to relate." [ll. 1–2]

Given besides the extremely tangential nature of the contact between narrator and old man, the supposed thoughts and images of the former in remembering the latter appear more than ever overextended—comically so in Carroll's version. That is, Wordsworth is so preoccupied with his own ruminations that the Leech-gatherer's

voice to me was like a stream
Scarce heard; nor word from word could I divide.
[ll. 107–108]

The White Knight, it is true, does divide the aged man's word from word, for

his answer trickled through my head,
Like water through a sieve. [ll. 7–8]

But of course the sense may be considered equally lost whether as an undifferentiated stream or drop by drop.

There is a certain presumptuousness in the "stranger's privilege" (l. 82) that Wordsworth takes in questioning the old man, especially since he pays so little attention to the answer. This aspect of the egotistical sublime is humorously transformed by Carroll. The aged man answers directly enough, with practical detail not unlike that in the Leech-gatherer's account of his steadily more difficult and less profitable employment. But since the White Knight doesn't listen, he doesn't hear, and therefore has no response but to repeat his question:

---

[6] The aura surrounding the Leech-gatherer may well be taken to illustrate that defect hit upon by Coleridge: "thoughts and images too great for the subject"; see *Biographia Literaria*, II, 109.

> So, having no reply to give
> To what the old man said,
> I cried, "Come tell me how you live!"
> And thumped him on the head. [ll. 21-24]

Or, a little later:

> I shook him well from side to side,
> Until his face was blue. [ll. 37-38]

The "I" of "Resolution and Independence" is a carefree and playful person, comparable in his lack of seriousness and responsibility to the landscape which opens the poem. This landscape is full of no-thought-for-the-future exuberance: the singing and chattering birds, the pleasant noise of waters, the "hare . . . running races in her mirth" and in her "joy" (ll. 11, 16); the very mist from the wet earth runs a long with the hare as if also racing. Wordsworth compares himself to the "playful hare" (l. 30): "Even such a happy Child of earth am I" (l. 31). His whole life has been lived "in pleasant thought" (l. 36). But Wordsworth is suddenly assailed by a doubt, whether all life's "business" can be a summer mood (l. 37). Can he continue to live so irresponsibly?

In the midst of this worry, the old man appears to Wordsworth. He is no lightsome creature like the hare, but one bowed under a "more than human weight" (l. 70). To Wordsworth he is like a messenger who will give him "human strength, by apt admonishment" (l. 112). The old man is going to tell Wordsworth how to live a human life. And he does so by answering the question, as phrased in the original version, " 'What kind of work [after 1815 changed to "occupation"] is that which you pursue?' " (l. 88). The Leech-gatherer's answer concerns "employments hazardous and wearisome" (l. 101), including "hardships to endure" (l. 102). Wordsworth is perplexed by the specters of "cold, pain, and labour" (l. 115), and seeks comfort from the Leech-gatherer, repeating his question, " 'How is it that you live, and what is it you do?' " (l. 119). The Leech-gatherer's answer is, " 'I persevere' " (l. 126). What this means on a literal level is: I keep on gathering leeches, no matter how they and their profitability dwindles. More metaphysically it means: I approach life not as play but as earnest duty and endurance.

Strange comfort! Does it mean Wordsworth stands admonished to abandon his carefree, playful life and resign himself to the more or less dreary (wandering about the "weary moors," always "alone and silent") (ll. 130–131), but more or less religiously sanctioned (giving "to God and man their dues") (l. 98) duty of work? If such a conclusion is intimated, however vaguely, it is a conclusion which Carroll is turning inside out in the White Knight's song. As William Empson observes, there is a shift of interest from the virtues of the aged man to those of his questioner in Carroll's parody.[7]

This is largely achieved through debasement of the aged aged man. In many respects the descriptions of the two old men tally. They both exhibit white hairs, mild looks, slow speech. But instead of "sable orbs," and "yet vivid eyes" (l. 91), Carroll gives the aged man "eyes, like cinders, all aglow" (l. 76). Instead of "courteous" (l. 86), and "stately" (l. 96) speech, "lofty utterance" (l. 94), "choice words and measured phrase" (l. 95), the aged man's words are

> muttered mumblingly and low,
> As if his mouth were full of dough. [ll. 79–80]

Worst of all, for the Leech-gatherer's "flash of mild surprise" (l. 90), the aged man "gave a wink" (l. 53).

Both the Leech-gatherer and the aged man are reporting how they make a living, the one by gathering leeches, the

---

[7] Empson, "Alice in Wonderland: The Child as Swain," in *Some Versions of Pastoral* (Norfolk, Conn., 1950), pp. 263–264; it is interesting also, as Empson points out, that most of the White Knight's inventions involve food.

other by gathering haddocks' eyes and hansom-cab wheels (among other occupations). Whatever for? is a question which is out of the question in Wordsworth's poem if it is to retain its serious tone, a question never far from mind in Carroll's, which throws that tone right out. Whatever he is doing —searching out butterflies to make mutton pies, digging for buttered rolls, setting limed twigs for crabs—the aged man, like the Leech-gatherer, perseveres. And as with the Leech-gatherer, his perseverance is not daunted even by disappointing returns:

> "Yet twopence-halfpenny is all
> They give me for my toil." [ll. 31–32]

Ever alert, ever striving to "get my bread" (l. 15), he doesn't lose a chance to beg or flatter a trifle of his interrogator, the White Knight.

If the aged man represents any "admonishment," it is to practicality, though a practicality of a most ignoble sort compared to that exalted in the Leech-gatherer. The only thing that makes the aged man's schemes practical is that they are undertaken for money. Otherwise they are as zany and as impossibly issueless as the schemes which run so perpetually and distractingly through the White Knight's head.

The circular nature of the Knight's plans is especially well demonstrated in the 1856 version. Here the narrator is

> thinking of a way
> To multiply by ten,
> And always, in the answer, get
> The question back again. [ll. 17–20]

Likewise, the White Knight thinks out a plan for dyeing one's whiskers green, then using a fan so large that this greenness won't be noticed (st. 3). The usefulness of feeding oneself on batter in order to get always a little fatter (st. 5) and the prac-

ticality of boiling the Menai bridge in wine to keep it from
rust (st. 8) are clearly nil, but the same can be said of the
aged man's toil. The activities of the two characters are virtually indistinguishable, except that in the one case they are undertaken for money, in the other for their own sake, just
because the White Knight likes thinking up plans.

He only finally hears the answer to his question when he has
completed one of his designs. What he has gotten from the
aged man remains ambiguous. He thanks the aged man for the
account of how he gets his wealth, but chiefly for

> his wish that he
> Might drink my noble health.   [ll. 63–64]

He is satisfied because he has completed something in his own
mind with the aged man as a sort of background. His resembles Wordsworth's satisfaction not so much with what the
Leech-gatherer actually says, but with what Wordsworth
imagines to himself as he says it.

Why and when should he White Knight ever think back
upon the aged aged man? The circumstances that remind him,
to the point of tears, are the following:

> And now, if e're by chance I put
> My fingers into glue,
> Or madly squeeze a right-hand foot
> Into a left-hand shoe,
> Or if I drop upon my toe
> A very heavy weight,
> I weep, for it reminds me so
> Of that old man I used to know—.   [ll. 65–72]

These incidents all concern absentminded ineptness. Do they
remind the White Knight of the aged man by contrast or
analogy? The whole song has thrown this into doubt. Besides,
given the minimal character of the old man and the extremely
tangential nature of their contact, what is there really for the

narrator to think of as he looks back? In Carroll's poem the White Knight doesn't even remember the old gate-sitter accurately; for example, he remarks near the end that the old man "seemed distracted with his woe" (l. 77), which is the first we hear of any such thing.

The White Knight's song comments by comic exaggeration on the non sequitur impact of the last line of Wordsworth's poem, " 'I'll think of the Leech-gatherer on the lonely moor!' " (l. 140). It demystifies and demeans the notion of toil for bread, along with the old man who preaches it. The poem may be taken as a sabotage of the ethic of perseverance in duty suggested by Wordsworth's "Resolution and Independence."[8]

[8] Perhaps thematically relevant is that Carroll composed another verse tangentially related to Wordsworth's "Resolution and Independence." This is a charade sent to Agnes Hull on Dec. 10, 1877, and mentioned in a letter to Maud Standen, Dec. 18, 1877, *Letters*, pp. 133–134, 74. Its first line echoes Wordsworth's, "They both make a roaring—a roaring all night." The poem has a stanza hinting at the word "sea," one at the word "son." The answer to the puzzle is "sea-son," on which the third stanza has this comment:

> Of the two put together, oh what shall I say?
> 'Tis a time when "to live" means the same as "to play."

The association of the reference to "Resolution and Independence" and the defining of living as playing is curiously supportive, I think, of the argument that the other parody, the White Knight's song, represents an undercutting of the stoic message recommending duty and endurance in "Resolution and Independence." It is commonly said that the White Knight is a self-portrait; for example, A. L. Taylor titles his biography *The White Knight: A Study of C. L. Dodgson* (Edinburgh, London, 1952). But Carroll also identifies himself as an "aged aged man" in a letter to Mary Brown of April 1, 1889, *Letters*, pp. 166–167, and also in "Isa's Visit to Oxford, 1888" (where the title is abbreviated as A. A. M), in *Diaries*, II, Appendix C, 557–561. These casual references suggest that Carroll recognized a certain similarity between himself and the aged man of the Knight's song. This might lie not only in the common factor of age (which Carroll liked to insist on when inviting adolescent girls to visit him), but also in their common addiction to work. (See Chapter 7 for a

And it throws into question a valuation which would place work higher than woolgathering and hobbyhorsing, that is, play.

Three Games and Their Tangled Ends

The White Knight's song celebrates play, or at least it knocks work on the head. And play—in the form of games— permeates the two *Alices*. Croquet, cards, and chess.

Carroll's own games may have played some part in the invention of the *Alices*. His version of croquet, Croquet Castles, apparently concocted at about the time he was concocting Alice's first adventures, is not especially remarkable. But it may be of some interest that he renders the game in military terminology; it is characterized by some of the truculence pervading Wonderland croquet. Carroll's card game, Court Circular, first printed in 1860 but reissued in simplified form in 1862, may also have been circulating in his mind in the July of that year, when he launched his tale during the famous river trip. Significant for *Alice's Adventures* in Court Circular is that the power hierarchy extends from the monarchs of hearts down, as per the order given in *Wonderland*, Chapter VIII. Also, Carroll emphasizes a rule that is of interest in relation to both *Alices*, that forbidding a player's resignation after a certain point in the game.[9] Some such rule is common in parlor games and is to be found often in *Hoyle*. Alice flaunts it in

---

brief discussion of Carroll's attitude toward work.) As the Knight's song suggests, work differs from nonwork or play not so much in its usefulness as in its more or less ulterior motivation.

[9] See Carroll, *Diaries*, I, 196; Collingwood, ed., *Diversions and Digressions*, p. 271; Carroll (Anonymous), "Croquet Castles" and "Rules for Court Circular," *Works*, pp. 1269–1271, 1265–1269; Carroll, *Alice's Adventures in Wonderland*, in *The Annotated Alice*, ed. Gardner; hereafter identified in the text as *W*, with page reference.

Chapter XII of Wonderland, when, in effect, she attempts to extricate herself from the game, which at that point is going against her badly. The question is: *can* Alice resign, and if she does, must she lose?

Because croquet and cards are important in *Alice in Wonderland*, one might expect them to be presiding or controlling structures. But this is not the case. The book does not so much show how everything fits into one or two inclusive systems, but how everything doesn't. For the terms of the game are lamentably unfixed as much in the card as in the croquet game. When balls turn into hedgehogs and mallets into flamingos, when caterpillars, cheshire cats, and mad hatters mix indiscriminately with cards of the standard deck, it is very hard to keep terms straight, let alone figure out the rules regulating their interplay.

The Looking-Glass game holds together only a bit better. Many of the characters do have identities as chesspieces. Alice herself fits into the scheme, though the same cannot be said of the Live Flowers, the Fawn, the Tweedle brothers, and others. Even the chesspieces are far from fixed; for instance, the White Queen turns into a Sheep. Though the moves may be represented on an actual chessboard, it is hard to understand what rule would prompt such a move, say, as W.Q. to Q.B. 8th, in which the White Queen flies from the Red Knight rather than simply taking him, as she would in the game as set forth by *Hoyle* and others. A show is made in the novel of elaborate coordination of narrative and game, and yet everything that happens cannot be understood in terms of the prefatory outline of the moves of the game.

Wonderland croquet and cards and Looking-Glass chess remain recognizable as games because enough terms and rules are in evidence to suggest that if just a few more could be ascertained, they must make up comfortable logical systems (and novels). Such a suggestion of overall rationality is what

Alice finds unrealized in the games she encounters in her adventures and what the reader, to the extent that he, like a child, expects sense instead of nonsense, finds unrealized in the parlor-games pseudostructures in the *Alices.*

As may be calculated from information given in *Looking-Glass,* Alice is respectively seven and seven and a half years old in the two novels (*L-G,* n. 1, p. 177). Two concerns are typical of children this age (I am using Piaget's categories in *The Language and Thought of the Child*) : concern for logical reasons for things, and concern for justification of rules. Children try "to connect everything to everything else." They are searching for a coherent universe. However, Alice does not find one, but multiple and shifting universes, each separate from the others. This is not to deny that there may be a kind of miniature rationality in any particular moment or interchange in the *Alices.* The jokes and puzzles, for instance, which make up so much of the novels, run on admirable logic, once one knows which logic is called for. Take "jam tomorrow and jam yesterday—but never jam to-day." Alice's common sense registers this as absurdity, but the logic of language supports it: "jam every *other* day: today isn't any *other* day, you know" (*L-G,* p. 247). The difficulty is that most of the time Alice can't tell what cosmos she is dealing with. She is always several steps behind whoever is choosing the grounds upon which the logic circulates. When she begins to catch up, they change systems on her. Because of this lack of fixity, Alice cannot rely on any encompassing coherence or consistency in Wonderland and Looking-Glass games. She is frustrated because, says W. H. Auden, "according to Lewis Carroll, what a child desires before anything else is that the world in which he finds himself should make sense. It is not the commands and prohibitions, as such, which adults impose that he resents, but rather that he cannot perceive any law linking one command to another in a consistent pattern." A dilemma like Alice's has been nicely summed up by T. E.

Hulme: "A line . . . seems about to unite the whole world logically. But the line stops. There is no unity. All logic and life are made up of tangled ends like that."[10]

Alice's movement through Wonderland and Looking-Glass land cannot be conceived as following a connected line, in spite of the linear continuity one might expect to find in narratives apparently organized upon parlor games. Rather, Alice bounces from universe to universe, each one moving in its own insulated round. When one is sucked into every game that happens to be near at hand, one is at a perpetual disadvantage. What Alice learns is something about making her own leaps of choice.

[10] Piaget, *The Language and Thought of the Child*, pp. 171f, 238; Auden, "Today's Wonder-World Needs Alice," *New York Times Magazine* (July 1962), p. 5; rprt. in *Aspects of Alice*, ed. Phillips, pp. 11, 9. Auden observes that in Wonderland Alice meets anarchy and incompetence, both incompatible with the play abounding in the novel; Hulme, "Cinders," in his *Speculations*, pp. 235–236.

4. Alice's Adventures in Wonderland

At the outset of *Alice in Wonderland*, Alice, somewhat bored with the book being read to her, considers amusing herself with a sort of play—making a daisy chain; she would do this for the fun of it, in spite of the trouble of getting up to pick the flowers. However, this type of play is not really what Alice prefers; typically, she likes social games, games with rules, of a more strictly structured character than is involved in daisy-chaining. Even when thrown back upon her solitary self, Alice is fond of pretending to be two people, so that, besides giving herself good advice, scolding herself to tears, she has also been known to play a game of croquet against herself (*W*, pp. 25, 32–33).

Given a choice, Alice would prefer to have other people around. As she falls down the rabbit hole, talking aloud to herself the while, she feel the absense of listeners, the opportunity of "showing off her knowledge." This suggests the importance of relative mastery in Alice's view of social relations, which are games insofar as they are undertaken out of the pure pleasure of competitive self-assertiveness. Language for Alice is to some extent a way of impressing others; she likes to say "latitude" and "longitude," without any notion of their meaning, but only because they are so satisfyingly "grand" to say. On the other hand, she reflects that a lack of knowledge of a word, for instance, having to ask an inhabitant of the other side of the globe what the name of his country is, would put her at a psychological disadvantage. She determines not to be caught out (*W*, pp. 27–28).

Alice has a game attitude, with which goes a great concern for the terms and rules of play. She is on the lookout to learn these so as to fit in and even master the peculiar universe she has entered. In the first chapter Alice's abiding interest in rules is introduced. For example, she remarks that she hopes to find a book of rules for shutting up like a telescope, and she recalls disapprovingly stories she has heard of children who had been burned and eaten up by wild beasts, "all because they *would* not remember the simple rules their friends had taught them." She is strict in her views about obeying rules. Once she even boxed her own ears for cheating at the croquet game she was playing with herself (*W*, pp. 30–33).

Alice entertains a self-satisfied, even smug opinion of herself as a rule-abiding little girl. In most cases the narrator's attitude is close to her own.[1] The possibility of great narrative distance or of narrative irony at the expense of the character is diminished by the fact that, as is sometimes suggested, Alice is listening and reacting to the narrator while living the adventures which he is at that moment relating. In one notable instance, just after the narrator remarks her fondness for pretending to be two people, Alice responds as if she had heard this: " 'But it's no use now . . . to pretend to be two people! Why, there's hardly enough of me left to make *one* respectable person!' " (*W*, p. 33).

However, the narrator does occasionally comment with some detachment on what Alice does, referring himself to the reader rather than to her. For example, he exclaims over her odd behavior while falling: "Fancy, *curtseying* as you're falling through the air! Do you think you could manage it?" (*W*, p.

---

[1] Cf. Harry Levin, "Wonderland Revisited," *Kenyon Review*, XXVII (Autumn 1965), 595: "No novelist has identified more intimately with the point of view of his heroine."

28). His description of her as the "wise little Alice" is one that Alice would be quite willing to accept; in fact she hears and responds to it: "It was all very well to say 'Drink me,' but the wise little Alice was not going to do *that* in a hurry. 'No, I'll look first,' she said, 'and see whether it's marked *'poison'* or not' " (*W*, p. 31). Still, the description may be taken by the reader, especially in conjunction with certain of the narrator's other descriptions, such as "this curious child" (*W*, p. 33), to be tinged with a judgment not so entirely favorable as Alice might assume.

One common reaction to Alice is that she is a bit of a prig. William Empson discusses the respect for conventions and desire to learn new ones which bring her close to snobbishness. Mark Van Doren comments, "Occasionally, perhaps regularly, she is treated like a little prig, a little girl who has no ability whatever to imagine other experiences than those she has had." One of the fullest investigations of this characteristic appears in Donald Rackin's study of *Alice in Wonderland.* In his assessment, Alice has reached a stage at which she believes that the world is explainable and unambiguous: "Daring curiosity is wedded to uncompromising literalness and priggish, ignorant faith in the fundamental sanity of all things. . . . She deals with the impossible as if it had to conform to the regular causal operations of her old world above ground." The judgment of these critics follows the lightly implied but irresistible critical judgment conveyed in the narration of *Alice in Wonderland.* It has something to do with Alice's solemn eagerness (an oversolemnity, and overeagerness, which she is to partly outgrow) to play whatever game is given by the powers that be. Alice flings herself down the rabbit hole out of curiosity and "never once considering" (*W*, p. 26). No matter what the game universe(s) she finds herself in, she is willing to go along. A poem by Robert Graves on Alice as a sort of national heroine is appreciative of her positive mindedness: "She set herself, with truly British pride / In being a pawn and playing for her side, / And simple faith in simple strategem, / To learn the rules and moves and perfect them." In my view, Alice's success in winning the game is not at all so perfect as Graves would have it, but prig-heroine as she is, she does accomplish something to be proud of.[2]

Alice is accustomed to a world in which "they" play a decisive part. "They" consist presumably of parental authorities and their delegates, nurses and governesses. For a little girl, the powers that be are primarily feminine. Alice recognizes her very subordinate position in relation to these powers, but she also knows it could be worse. She is especially concerned to convince herself (by the testimony of her hair and her command of lessons) that she is still herself. For to be Mabel, say, would entail a great deal more unpleasant infringement upon her personal sphere than she has ever had to submit to. That is, she would have to live in a poky house, possess "next to no toys to play with," and suffer extra lessons. The thought of being that low in the power structure (remember Carroll's outline of an intolerable existence consisting only of meals and lessons, no play at all), without even a realm of one's own toys to reign in, induces a rebellious fantasy in Alice: " 'No, I've made up my mind about it: if I'm Mabel, I'll stay down here! It'll be no use their putting their heads down and saying, "Come up again, dear!" I shall only look up and say,

---

[2] Empson, "The Child as Swain," in *Some Visions of Pastoral*, p. 278; Van Doren, ed., "Lewis Carroll, *Alice in Wonderland*," in *The New Invitation to Learning*, p. 121; Rackin, "Alice's Journey to the End of Night," *PMLA*, LXXXI (Oct. 1966), 314; Graves, "Alice," *Collected Poems* (Garden City, 1961), p. 59, rprt. in *Aspects of Alice*, ed. Phillips, pp. 114–115. Also, for a fine survey of critical approaches to *Alice in Wonderland* see Rackin, "The Critical Interpretations of Alice in Wonderland: A Survey and Suggested Reading" (dissertation University of Illinois, 1964). He treats *Alice*: as personal revelation, biographical and psychological approaches; as topical satire and allegory; as technical text, mathematical, logical, and linguistic approaches; as game (Sewell); as myth—his own approach.

"Who am I, then? Tell me that first, and then, if I like being that person, I'll come up: if not, I'll stay down here till I'm somebody else"'—" But the passage ends with the collapse of the rebel: " 'Oh dear!' cried Alice, with a sudden burst of tears, 'I do wish they would put their heads down! I am so *very* tired of being all alone here!' " (*W*, pp. 38–39).

Alice prefers society (and its games) to solitude, even if society consists of authorities on one side, establishing all the givens, and herself on the other, accepting and obeying them. She does not dispute the principle enunciated by the Lory, that he who is older knows best—she only wants to make certain he is really older (*W*, p. 45). Alice accepts a world of "Rules and Regulations," as in Carroll's early poem of that name. The moral of the piece is "Behave." It teaches how to "avoid dejection" by various "occupations," "recreations." These include domineering over those one can: "Starve your canaries," "Be rude to strangers," while all the time realizing that there are limits to one's powers:

> Don't push with your shoulder
> Until you are older.[3]

Alice does not follow out the opportunity suggested in her fantasy to escape authorities and rules underground. She brings with her respect and submissiveness to them, even remembering, for instance, to address the Mouse according to a rule that she had gleaned out of someone else's book and never had occasion to use herself, namely, the rule governing address in Latin: " 'O Mouse!' " Note too her adherence to the principle of penalty to him who breaks a rule. When there is no

[3] Carroll, from *Useful and Instructive Poetry* (1845), introd. Derek Hudson (London, 1954), pp. 38–40, rprt. in *The Humorous Verse of Lewis Carroll, The Rev. Charles Lutwidge Dodgson*, illus. Sir John Tenniel, Arthur B. Frost, Henry Holiday, Harry Furniss, unabridged republication of *The Collected Verse of Lewis Carroll* (London, 1933), (New York, 1960), pp. 10–11.

one else to do it, she accepts without a trace of resentment the notion of being "punished" for her trespass of crying, by drowning in her own tears (*W*, pp. 36, 40–41).

In Chapter II the only person that Alice condemns with her strongest word of disapproval—nonsense—is herself. One piece of nonsense that issues from her mouth is the poem, "How doth the little crocodile." However, this makes a good deal of sense in terms of the ruthless world she has entered (not to mention the one she has left).[4] That is, the pious idea of the original by Isaac Watts concerning the busy bee who improves each shining hour with books, work, or "healthful play" has been stripped of its piety. For as the busy bee gathers food, so likewise does the crocodile, but instead of honey, fishes. There is no talk of improving use of time in his case, but of direct self-improvement—by eating (*W*, p. 38, and n. 4, pp. 38–39). So self-interest rather than altruism is exposed as a basic motive; and self-interest is clearly represented as antithetical to others' interests. Wonderland is a crocodile-eat-fish world which puts the lie to the many moralistic children's lessonbook verses that Alice is accustomed to recite, but that simply won't come right underground. What is more, as this poem perhaps intimates, one creature may eat another not out of need (hunger) but for fun (play).

The first proper game in which Alice participates underground is the caucus-race. What characterizes this race is the lack of clear rules. That is, the play area is vaguely defined— "a sort of circle ('the exact shape doesn't matter')." There is no one starting point for the runners. They begin at no fixed

---

[4] *Alice's Adventures* says something about the real world and about Alice herself. For an excellent discussion of the implications of the fact that the dream is after all Alice's, with all its oral aggressiveness, see Nina Auerbach, "Alice and Wonderland: A Curious Child," Victorian Child issue, *Victorian Studies*, XVII (1973), 31–47. Auerbach reminds us that Alice stands out among the girl characters of Victorian fiction because she is by no means simply an embodiment of sweet innocence.

moment, and they leave off when they like. In effect, this is an egocentric kind of play, where everyone does as he likes, and yet the game is social in that it includes the notion of competition and winning. Its two aspects—of chaotic freedom and of ordered ranking of outcomes—are incompatible. The latter cannot follow from the former; therefore the solution: " 'Everybody has won, and *all* must have prizes' " (*W*, pp. 48–50).

Play bears an interesting relation to utility in the caucus-race. The animals run to get dry after their soaking in the pool of tears. The running as such is not play, as it is motivated by need, but the race structure is, as it is quite unnecessary. Thus the prize is not succeeding in getting dry (fulfillment of the original purpose) but a formal token. In this case, appropriately in terms of the incorporation model I have been invoking, the prize is something to eat, one of Alice's comfits.

In all, this race demonstrates the arbitrary nature of winning. One wins when the rules say so, the rules being issued unilaterally by the Dodo. The race is over when the Dodo announces it's over. And the shape that the race takes also demonstrates something characteristic about games: their circularity. In spite of all the purposiveness displayed by the players (a displaced purposiveness as already pointed out) the game literally does not get anyone anywhere. Or, to qualify, the only place a game gets you is in front of your opponent, except this one doesn't because, like so many in Wonderland, it is not quite a proper game, after all. And Alice isn't too happy about that.

Another more sinister system with something of a game structure is that of the trial, as presented in the "Mouse's Tale," which in a sense forecasts what is to come in the *Adventures*. Fury, like the Dodo in the caucus-race, makes all the rules, and what is more, compels the other player to play. There is merely an illusion of reciprocity, given by the line, " 'Let us both go to law.' " Actually, the power and the will to play are all on one side; the Mouse has no choice. Fury is prosecutor, judge, and jury, and condemns the Mouse to death. Fury may be said to be playing in that he undertakes the trial out of whim, " 'For really this morning I've nothing to do' " (*W*, p. 51). Whether in such a cat and mouse game the mouse is playing is very doubtful. Free choice is essential to the play spirit. What we may have here is something Carroll calls "sport," to be investigated in Chapter 6.

Alice somewhat resembles the Mouse in that she allows herself to be put upon and ordered about in the various Wonderland games, virtually none of which turns out to be at all to her advantage. But the difference is that she chooses (up to a certain point) to submit, freely to enter game systems for which presumably someone else has defined the terms, made the rules.

For example, Alice thinks the whole affair of the caucus-race "absurd," but it is characteristic of her attitude, at this point at least, that since everyone else takes it seriously, she suppresses her urge to laugh (which would disrupt the system through breach of implicit faith)—she plays along. In fact, she is very solicitous, afraid of offending, apologetic for having spoken what the Mouse considers "nonsense" (*W*, pp. 49–50, 52). Interestingly, she does not directly refuse to go along with what the creatures expect of her; her only form of resistance is an indirect threat, through ostensibly unthinking references to Dinah the cat and her penchant for eating mice and birds (as if to say, I may be weak, but I have someone at home who could eat you up).

I have gone on at some length about the caucus-race because it is the first game Alice meets, if not entirely a proper one. Let me go on a little longer to discuss another interpretation of the race and its implications—jumping ahead of ourselves now—for both *Alices*. This is the chapter on the *Alices* in Roger Henkle's "Comedies of Liberation." I want to point out where I take exception to Henkle: I think the caucus-race is on the far side of games along the play-games-sport line, whereas Henkle places it on the near. Still, his piece is one of the best things one can read if interested in play and Carroll.

Henkle postulates an idyll of "free play," supposed to be the original condition presented in *Wonderland*, where each creature determines his life solely by whim and self-indulgence. The action of both novels involves the fall from this condition. According to Henkle, play is one's own order, to be changed if desired: "Play is continuing at what you like (or think you like) doing best, and being safe and undisturbed while doing it." It offers "the appeal of a routine in which you can set your own rules, begin and leave off when you like, and be immune temporarily from the incursions of others."[5]

Henkle defines play to mean basically free play (we may understand this as Piaget's first two stages), so that more restrictive games with rules appear as fallings off from the ideal. In trying to show that an idyllic condition of free play originally exists, he points to the caucus-race, where everybody does what he likes and all win. The croquet match and, worse, the trial are then seen as perversions of the "joyously free caucus-race kind of game."[6]

[5] Henkle, "Comedies of Liberation: A Study of Meredith, Carroll, and Butler" (dissertation Stanford University, 1968), pp. 22, 32, 56–57, 23, 55. Henkle's essential ideas appear also in "The Mad Hatter's World," *Virginia Quarterly Review*, IL (1973), 99–117. Again, my differences with his interpretation are two: he defines play in its primitive form and seems almost to deny that games are play; he observes that play as he defines it cannot last in Carroll's novels, but explains their demise by their vulnerability to violence that is outside rather than part of the play impulse itself. See too James R. Kincaid, "Alice's Invasion of Wonderland," *PMLA*, LXXXVIII (1973), 92–99; he finds Alice an invader disrupting a warm and happy world, the caucus-race and the tea-party representing for him, as for Henkle, the "joyous side of anarchy."

[6] Henkle, "Comedies of Liberation," pp. 22, 58, 27; Gattegno, *Lewis Carroll*, p. 209, sets Alice consistently at an intellectual level above the creatures, claiming that she demands rule-games, they are content with the earliest type, solitary games without rules.

But does this contrast hold up very well? The caucus-race is after all a contest, and it is marked out and directed, solo, by the Dodo. The creatures all want to win (beat the others?), though such a concept would be foreign to truly precompetitive play. Alice, far from being "joyous" about the fact that everyone gets to win, is "in despair." For that matter, it is not at all certain that she is joyously free and doing what she wants when she joins the race. Out of politeness she asks, " 'What *is* a Caucus-race?' . . . not that she much wanted to know" (*W*, pp. 48–49). There exists a significant element of imposition here; Alice is little more "immune . . . from the incursions of others" in this game than in any other in the novels. She more or less willingly submits to play, as is usual in rule games.

If Piaget is correct, the individual does not lay down rules as such for his private egocentric play, except maybe by analogy to those he has been given in regular rule games. Rules are meaningless except in competitive or at least socialized play, where each player agrees to be to some extent rulebound. The notion and the word "rule" occur frequently throughout the *Alices*, which argues an emphasis upon games with rules rather than upon free play. Certainly, rule-consciousness is entrenched in Alice, as shown beginning with the first chapter. This consciousness likewise pervades the other characters in the books. The creatures may enjoy "a routine in which you can set your own rules," but they expect others to obey them.

A lack of stable rule-structure plagues Wonderland (and Looking-Glass land), but this does not ensure that the player will be immune from others' incursions. It gives him less, not more security against being imposed upon, and this is as true in the caucus-race as later in the croquet game. Henkle invokes a prerule definition of play as a norm. In a sense, the White Knight's song celebrates a generalized concept of play, but it is one contrasted to work, not to games. Although in certain works Carroll seems to lament the turning of games into sport, as I hope to show, it is risky to theorize that he must also lament the turning of free play into games. The *Alice* narratives do not appear to offer good enough or many enough instances of primitive play to make this a valid point of reference in discussing the novels.

The world Alice enters does not operate according to mental structures of an age younger than herself—an innocent and flamboyant realm of presocialized freedom and unrule-bound self-expression. If this were the case the creatures would not be so insistent on her submission to their games. Rather this world represents an older level of mental organization, characterized by an addiction to games with rules, with which Alice is expected to play along.

The Queen of Hearts is an extreme example of a general tendency to domineer and not an exception, as Henkle would have it. His thesis rests upon a distinction that would identify the Mad Hatter as well as the caucus-racers with free-play egocentrism which does not impose on others, and the Queen with rule-game extension (and, he implies perversion) of such egotism, which is expressed not only in living by whim but in imposing its whim on others.[7] But, if I may point ahead here,

---

[7] Henkle, "Comedies of Liberation," pp. 23–24. Albert Cook's formulation is somewhat similar to Henkle's although it does not employ the concept of play (*The Dark Voyage and the Golden Mean*, pp. 125–132). His comments on Carroll are based on a theory of the "desire for the nonprobable" in the face of the closing in the probable in all social life. Hence *Alice in Wonderland* is a comedy of the confrontation between the wonder of childhood and the unwonderful predictability of adulthood. Whether the novel represents the socialization of Alice is not clear from Cook's discussion, as his treatment of the book is sketchy in comparison with his psychoanalytic speculations on what the book reveals about Carroll. Another interpretation more closely resembles Henkle's in estimating "*Alice* as one more sick Victorian cry in the night against the monstrous encroachment of adolescence on the purity and innocence of childhood." This view is expressed in Malcolm Muggeridge's review of Jonathon Miller's

isn't the Mad Hatter as much a bully in his way as the Queen of Hearts (or the Red Queen)? Certainly his egotism expresses itself via social contact. I cannot agree with Henkle that the self-assertion of the Queen operates as a threat to a carefree anarchy of happily coexisting, minimally interacting free players, thereby killing free individual action and necessitating social restraints. The creatures impinge on one another all along. This is obvious in the perpetual battling and contests, verbal and physical. Play in the *Alices* is always interplay, usually violent.

Let us go forward now with *Alice's Adventures*. In the rough interplay of Wonderland, Alice is content, initially, to put up with a hard time. She is acquiescent and accepts a very humble position: she is mistaken for the housemaid by the White Rabbit and goes on an errand for him. This is as strange as if at home, besides having to submit to the normal authorities, she were to be ordered about by animals, the very cat. Alice imagines being ordered by Dinah to watch a mousehole. She supposes though that at home she could count on some protection against such servitude, from the same "them" who are the usual authorities (*W*, p. 56). Alice even wishes she were back home, where besides being sure of one's size one isn't "ordered about by mice and rabbits." " 'I almost wish I hadn't gone down that rabbit hole,' " she adds, " 'and yet—and yet' " (*W*, p. 58). After all, Alice is willing to stick it out. She still wants to see the lovely garden, and can't resist the very curiousness of this new world. So she chooses to go

---

television movie of *Alice in Wonderland*, "Alice Where Art Thou?" *New Statesman*, LXXII (Dec. 23, 1966), 933. However, Miller visualizes the creatures as decadent adults, "under the cool disdainful gaze of the child," while Henkle sees them as not yet socialized beings and Alice as relatively adult. The movie dispenses with the card framework altogether. I cannot but feel that this must be a significant loss, although I haven't seen the show. See John Coleman's review, "Disheveled Dream-scape," *New Statesman*, LXXII (Dec. 23, 1966), 947.

on in her subordinate role. She trembles at the White Rabbit's voice, though in actual fact she is a thousand times his size and has no need to be afraid (*W*, p. 59). And later, once out of the Rabbit's house and much reduced in size, she fears being eaten by the puppy. Her encounter with him resembles "having a game of play with a cart horse" (*W*, p. 65). In all the games she enters into in Wonderland, Alice labors under a disadvantage of about this proportion.

On several occasions she feels the disadvantage quite strongly, as for example in the Caterpillar encounter. She hates being contradicted and feels she's losing her temper, and yet she swallows it down and maintains her politeness (*W*, p. 72). Consider also this instance of Alice's really heroic considerateness of others in the face of the signal lack of anyone's consideration for herself: though one of her great desires has been to achieve and stabilize her natural size, she actually shrinks herself to a diminutive nine inches before approaching the Duchess's house, because " 'it'll never do to come upon them *this* size: why, I should frighten them out of their wits!' " (*W*, p. 78).

"Pig and Pepper" is a chapter largely about will, or willfulness. Alice notes to herself how dreadfully all the Wonderland creatures argue. The song sung by the Duchess to the baby is in all probability a parody of a poem which teaches:

> Speak gently! It is better far
> To rule by love than fear.

The original is all about curbing one's outspoken urgency into gentleness. The Duchess's song, on the other hand, recommends an unleashed battle of wills, which assumes that one's little boy's willfulness is not to be coaxed and tamed but quite simply overpowered:

> Speak roughly to your little boy,
> And beat him when he sneezes:

He only does it to annoy,
Because he knows it teases. [*W*, p. 85 and n. 3] [8]

The Duchess's remedy for insurgency is capital punishment (*W*, p. 84).

Alice, as we have seen, is not very assertive of her own will but rather seeks direction from others. The chapter opens with her "wondering what to do next" (*W*, p. 79). The creatures she encounters refuse to be of much help. The advice received from the Caterpillar, for example, had been excessively cryptic (*W*, p. 73). And now the Frog-Footman remains obdurately unhelpful when Alice begs to know, " 'But what am I to do!' " At last she does take the initiative, and dismissing the Frog-Footman as "perfectly idiotic," she opens the door herself and walks into the Duchess's house. Still she has not yet learned much about willfulness as she remains "timid" with the Duchess, afraid of displaying a lack of "good manners" in presuming to begin the conversation herself (*W*, pp. 81–83).

With the Cheshire Cat she is equally timid. She inquires like a dutiful child, " 'Would you tell me, please, which way I ought to go from here?' " But the Cheshire Cat is as perverse as the Footman in refusing to give Alice the direction she wants. He throws the question back to her: " 'That depends a good deal on where you want to get to!' " Alice doesn't know where she wants to go; she says she doesn't much care. But she adds, " 'so long as I get somewhere.' " She wants a goal, and she wants someone else to set it for her. This need is not satisfied by the Cat's response: that she can go any way she likes, that it doesn't matter which way she goes, as no matter whom she goes among will be mad (*W*, pp. 88–89). Alice is very reluctant to go among mad people and even more so to be told she must be mad too, for being in Won-

[8] See also John Mackay Shaw, *The Parodies of Lewis Carroll and Their Originals*, catalog of an exhibition with notes (Florida State University, 1960).

derland. As a polite, well-lessoned little girl, she stakes a lot on her sanity.

At this juncture she is saved from directionlessness, though, for the Cheshire Cat mentions the Queen's croquet game, which Alice would like very much to attend (if asked). The Cat intimates an invitation by remarking, " 'You'll see me there' " (*W*, p. 89). Now at midpoint in the book, Alice receives the clearest goal she has had yet. She does not make or even actively choose her own game universe, but she is eager to join in any that offers, once fairly invited.

The Mad Tea-Party shows again Alice's interest in where activities lead, where they get to. She finds these mad creatures with their endless circulating around the tea table very incompatible. Alice asks the embarrassing question, which the Mad Hatter does not choose to answer, what happens when you arrive back at your original place? This concern to know where it will all end is typical of the game-playing mentality, which conceives activity as linear, as going from point X to point Y. But given the infinite extensibility of most processes, or their circular nature, which yields a similar inconclusiveness (as seen in the caucus-race as well as in the Mad Tea Party), a stop rule is absolutely necessary. The stop rule is what Alice wants to know.

Alice likes riddles; she is eager and determined to apply herself, but not to such as the Mad Hatter asks, because she feels that riddles without answers are a waste of her time (*W*, pp. 95, 97). Though the game, the riddle, is quite literally a waste of time in terms of practical use, it is felt as a waste in psychological terms if it does not allow of a solution, a gratifying sense of closure and triumph. Play activity begins arbitrarily; it is simple enough to begin drawing everything that starts with an M, as the three sisters undertake to do in the Dormouse's story. " 'Why with an M?' said Alice. 'Why not?' said the March Hare" (*W*, p. 103). One might, with ingenuity, find a way to draw mousetraps, moon, memory, muchness, etc. (It's all in how one defines terms, sets up rules.) But perhaps Alice has another doubt concerning this enterprise—how could one ever leave off drawing things that begin with an M? In any event, Alice alternates between an attempt to play along civilly with the Tea-Partyers, and dismay at their outrageousness. At one point she promises "humbly" not to interrupt the Dormouse again. And yet this is in apology for speaking "very angrily" to him. She overlooks the Hatter's calling her "stupid," but this after accusing him of rudeness and after snapping at him sharply (*W*, pp. 101, 102, 94). Finally she cannot bear their provocations and walks off in disgust, although, interestingly, she somewhat regrets this bold action, as she keeps looking back "half hoping that they would call after her." Only when they show no signs of wanting her back does she denounce them (to herself) once and for all: " 'At any rate I'll never go *there* again;' said Alice. . . . "It's the stupidest tea-party I ever was at in all my life!' " (*W*, pp. 103–104).

Alice thus demonstrates some capacity to reject past destinations of her own accord, though she cannot as yet propose future ones on the strength of her own will. However, given a purpose, she is persistent in working to achieve it. She does finally get into the garden where the croquet match is being held.

At the start of "The Queen's Croquet-Ground" Alice exhibits increased self-confidence and unwillingness to defer to others. Though she is polite to the Queen, she remarks to herself, " 'They're only a pack of cards, after all. I needn't be afraid of them!' " She disclaims responsibility for the situation in which she has merely happened to become involved, the dilemma of the three spade-card gardeners. And when the Queen attempts to enforce her responsibility by punishing her, Alice silences the Queen with a " 'Nonsense.' " Apparently she is allowed to get away with this impertinence because she is "only a child," no serious threat to the card world (*W*, pp. 108–109).

Alice is on no one's side now, but only standing up for herself. She is anything but deferential, laughing to hear that the Duchess has boxed the Queen's ears, and without pity at learning of the Duchess's scheduled execution for that act (*W*, p. 111).

The croquet game itself typifies the games of Wonderland. It frustrates Alice because of the maddening absence of fixity in rules or terms: " 'I don't think they play at all fairly,' Alice began, in rather a complaining tone, 'and they all quarrel so dreadfully one can't hear oneself speak—and they don't seem to have any rules in particular: at least, if there are, nobody attends to them—and you've no idea how confusing it is all the things being alive: for instance, there's the arch I've got to go through next walking about at the other end of the ground—and I should have croqueted the Queen's hedgehog just now, only it ran away when it saw mine coming!' " (*W*, p. 113). The rules are not only confusing or altogether lacking, but self-contradictory. For example, as far as Alice can see, there is no waiting for turns, and still the Queen decrees execution for missing a turn (*W*, pp. 112, 115). The coherence essential to a game is impossible.

Since the pieces, or terms, in the game are alive and ever-transforming or escaping, they cannot contribute the necessary definition and reliability. The flamingos keep twisting temperamentally about, the hedgehogs run off to fight with each other, and the soldiers walk away from their positions as arches to remove participants condemned by the Queen. Because of the complete devastation of the playing field and the players, the game can never be concluded (*W*, p. 124).

The soldier/arches provide a good example of the definition of terms by attributes and the interrelation of terms and rules in a game. When they are arches they are defined according to a rule of relationship to the rest of the game: fixed positions through which the balls must be struck in a certain sequence in order to win. But when they are soldiers they are defined according to the rule: those who do the Queen's bidding and who arrest those she accuses.

For similar fluctuations in terms according to their attributes, and consequent fluctuations in the rules governing them, we may remember Alice as little girl/serpent, the fish/footman, the baby/pig. It doesn't matter to the Pigeon what Alice is per se, but only what her attributes are. Both a serpent and a little girl "eat eggs"; therefore in the Pigeon's mind they are equivalent terms, both governed by an obnoxious rule of behavior (*W*, pp. 76–77). Judging by his face, Alice would have taken the creature she meets outside the Duchess's door to be a fish (presumably he should act according to fish rules), but since he is in livery, she defines him as a footman, and expects him to act accordingly (*W*, pp. 79–80). As a baby, the creature in Alice's arms should not exhibit the attributes of "grunting," but as a pig it displays this attribute quite properly and according to rule (*W*, p. 87).

Wonderland is a game world which ostensibly values definition and clarity, although it signally fails to achieve these. The Duchess congratulates Alice for her clear way of putting things (in particular, her ability to distinguish between mustard and a bird, something that is beyond the Duchess's power). The Duchess's own precept is "Be what you would seem to be," but she, like other Wonderland characters, has a fatal penchant for confusion, with the result of total incoherence: " 'Never imagine yourself not to be otherwise than what it might appear to others that what you were or might have been was not otherwise than what you had been would have appeared to them to be otherwise' " (*W*, pp. 121–122).

Terms and rules must remain constant if one is to know what universe one is dealing with. The croquet game does not meet this criterion. Two of the basic requirements for play as formulated in game theory are lacking: (1) Alice is not cognizant of all the terms and rules, and (2) therefore she cannot play rationally (maximize utility or undertake to play a winning strategy). "Alice soon came to the conclusion that it was a very difficult game indeed" (*W*, p. 112). And though it is impossible to play correctly, the penalty is great for a false move, as the whole spirit of this game is one of capital risk. Alice is getting uneasy. Though she had previously displayed some bravado in saying "Nonsense" to the Queen and recalling that she needn't fear mere cards, she is being ordered about more than ever in her life before, and she fears a dispute with the Queen, for then, " 'What would become of me?' " (*W*, pp. 125, 112).

Wonderland is a competitive, have and have-not world, as in the Duchess's moral: "The more there is of mine, the less there is of yours." What makes the world go round?—minding one's own business, which, as far as the Duchess is concerned, amounts to the same thing as love (*W*, pp. 122, 120–121). For her, love means self-love.

Because she is dealing with such a world, Alice feels it politic to flatter the Queen; what she says has a certain sinister accuracy, namely, the Queen is so likely to win, it's hardly worth finishing the game (*W*, p. 114). The Queen may not be able to win at croquet, strictly speaking, through lack of opponents to finish up (unless perhaps they may be considered to forfeit upon disappearing from the game). But she may be playing at something simpler: another version of Fury and the Mouse. (Carroll describes the Red Queen of *Looking-Glass* in " 'Alice' on the Stage" as "a sort of embodiment of ungovernable passion—a blind and aimless Fury," and the Queen of Hearts is not far different.) It is no wonder that Alice chooses to escape this game. The threat of losing one's head is literally and according to the common idiom the threat of losing all control.[9]

[9] Carroll, " 'Alice' on the Stage," from *The Theatre* (April 1887), rprt.

In spite of herself, Alice is still eager enough to believe that the systems she encounters will be decipherable, rational. Her reasoning goes something as follows: it is true, the creatures assume authority over me in the most galling manner and order me about as if I were at lessons, but if I can figure out by observation (certainly no one bothers to clue me in) the terms and rules by which the system operates, then when I'm in power (I'm only a little girl now, but bound to grow up someday), I'll be able to employ them according to my will, in effect, enjoy the pleasures of mastery.

It is typical of Alice to be very "much pleased at having found out a new kind of rule." " 'Maybe it's always pepper that makes people hot-tempered . . . and vinegar that makes them sour—and camomile that makes them bitter—and—and barley sugar and such things that make children sweet-tempered' " (*W*, pp. 119–120). Alice plans how she will manage things when *she's* a Duchess.

So Alice's faith in rational games persists. Her quickness in figuring out a sequence according to implied rules and her concern for what happens at the end are demonstrated by her questioning of the Mock Turtle, who did ten hours of lessons the first day, nine the second, and so on (which is why they are called lessons). Alice finds this a curious plan and is intrigued enough to figure that " 'the eleventh day must have been a holiday?' " " 'And how did you manage on the twelfth?' " But the Mock Turtle, like the Mad Hatter, turns the conversation, frustrating Alice of a definite stop rule and clear outcome (*W*, p. 130).

Of special interest about the Lobster Quadrille is that it is specifically identified as a game (*W*, pp. 130–131). This emphasizes again the basic circularity, the real pointlessness of play, which like a dance is primitively more of a here-we-go-

---

in Collingwood, ed., *Diversions and Digressions*, p. 171; see Henkle, "Comedies of Liberation," p. 72, and Greenacre, *Swift and Carroll*, pp. 243–244.

round-and-round activity than a getting-somewhere activity, though as we have seen, competitive games parade a certain point-X to point-Y linearity, where in practical terms point Y is not anymore somewhere than point X except that one player gets there first. And the only practicality in games is that of the pleasure they produce, the pleasure of final victory in a game nine times out of ten replacing the pleasure of step-by-step in a dance. Alice does not have much sympathy for the latter; it makes her nervous.

The Gryphon and Mock Turtle dance "round and round Alice" while they sing their very symmetrical refrain:

> Will you, won't you, will you, won't you,
>> Will you join the dance?
> Will you, won't you, will you, won't you,
>> Won't you join the dance?

But she has a strongly developed time and direction sense and really dislikes the infinity threatened by such circularity. She feels "very glad that it was over at last" (*W*, pp. 133–135).

Alice had still been allowing herself to be reprimanded for "nonsense" in Chapter X, but in Chapter XI she begins to show a good deal less docility under abuse.

She is pleased with herself for being able to identify all the figures at the trial, for example, the judge because he has a wig (again, a term defined by its attribute with an implied rule of proper function). She is pleased because she knows the word "jurors." The jurors themselves, on the other hand, are so bad at clear definition of terms that they are afraid of forgetting their own names. This makes Alice indignant, and she calls them "stupid things." She cannot bear the jurors' incapacity; a squeaking pencil is the last straw. So she takes away the offending object. Alice is becoming self-assured and bold (*W*, pp. 144–145).

The White Rabbit is a sort of master of ceremonies and tries to insist on the rules to be observed in court, for instance,

by giving the King whispered instructions. He is quite in-
effectual, but Alice is still curious to see what will come of the
proceedings. Apparently, " 'though they haven't much evidence
yet,' " she thinks they might manage it in the long run (*W*,
pp. 146, 151–152).

Alice is growing. Increase in size correlates with increase in
boldness. Always before a food or drink had caused her to
grow; this time she is in some sense doing it on her own.
Whereas in the past, for example in the White Rabbit's house,
large size had not mitigated an irrational timidity, now it represents and reinforces a larger courage. True, she is at first still
meek:" 'I can't help it [if] I'm growing.' " But then more boldly
she answers the Dormouse—" 'Don't talk nonsense' "—about
having no right to grow. Alice is simply assuming more rights.
With her increased power she is no longer trapped in any
situation where she might not choose to remain. It would no
longer be a matter of escape for her to leave, but of simply
walking out. Nevertheless, she *decides* to stay (*W*, pp. 147–
148).

The last chapter shows Alice in her final transformation
from assiduous and obedient aspirant, intent on working her
way up from the bottom toward command of the system; now
she is rebel and overthrower of that system. Though surprised,
she is willing to respond to the call to give evidence, and she
is dismayed, apologetic, at accidentally upsetting the jurybox;
she is even solicitous for the jurymen's lives. She obeys the
King's order to put them back in their places, and yet observes
that it wouldn't much matter whether they went in feet or
head first. Likewise, she remarks, " 'It doesn't matter a bit' "
which way the jury writes down a piece of evidence, as both
are equally meaningness (*W*, pp. 153–156).

Alice's increasing rebelliousness climaxes in actual revolt
when "Rule Forty-two" is invoked against her: "All persons
more than a mile high to leave the court." She refuses to go for
three reasons: (1) she is not a mile high, not in the category of

those to whom the rule might apply and hence not bound by it; (2) it is not a regular rule, but just invented, hence not binding; (3) " 'I shan't go, at any rate.' " The third is perhaps the most significant reason, as it implies: even if your game were coherent and consistent, which it isn't, I shouldn't have to play it unless I chose, which I don't (*W*, p. 156).

This time Alice does not simply remove herself from the game, which would leave the game itself intact. Instead she actively disrupts it. She declares the evidence meaningless (because of the ambiguity and confusion of terms caused by vague pronoun reference in the poem attributed to the Knave of Hearts), and she refuses to hold her tongue (*W*, pp. 158–159). Alice is now so large that she is completely unafraid, and a palpable threat to the court. She challenges it with a loud " 'Stuff and Nonsense,' " and declares for the second time, but now out loud rather than harmlessly to herself, " 'Who cares for *you*. . . . You're nothing but a pack of cards!' " (*W*, p. 161). The game must destroy or evict her, for it cannot maintain itself in the disruptive presence of a spoilsport.[10] This is what Alice has learned to be, through her lessons in frustration and her increasing awareness of the foundation of play systems upon pure will. Alice is beginning to recognize the rudiments of a Fury-and-the-Mouse model—in the unilateral proclamations of the Dodo, in the outrageous answerless riddles of the Mad Hatter, in the shifting terms and rules of a capital-risk croquet that renders the Queen of Hearts sure to win, and now in a court that invents laws as it goes, and against Alice. If terms, rules, and whole games are founded upon fiat—why not hers as well as theirs? Volition remains to Alice; she is not finally a Mouse.

[10] See Huizinga, *Homo Ludens*, p. 11: "The spoil-sport shatters the play-world itself. By withdrawing from the game he reveals the relativity and fragility of the play-world in which he had temporarily shut himself with others." This is why he is much less tolerated by other players even than the cheat.

But the end of *Wonderland* is difficult to interpret. Does Alice succeed in destroying the game? Or does it succeed in evicting her, by ejecting her from her dream? She challenges the cards, but it is they who fly at her (*W*, p. 161). I tend toward the former interpretation. As Piaget points out, play and dream are related, as they are both the ego's strategies of incorporating reality. But more control is maintained in play, for one remains aware of its voluntary status and the fact that one can end it when one chooses. In a dream the nightmare might very well continue indefinitely, for one cannot will to wake up.[11] However, one can will not to play, even in a dream, and thus end the nightmare, if it consists of a game world, by ending the game. This is what Alice does; hers is the initiative. I agree in a certain sense with Empson's statement that "the triumphant close of *Wonderland* is that she [Alice] has outgrown her fancies and can afford to wake and despise them," except that I would add that it is the choosing not to play others' mad games that wakes her.[12]

The end is a triumph insofar as Alice extricates herself from the game world altogether. To a true spoilsport, none of the rules of the game apply, even the rule, a common insurance of the inviolability of parlor games, which says that willful displacement of the pieces forfeits the game.[13] One must be very strong-minded to abolish the nagging compulsion of such a rule. But Alice has developed into a very strong-minded little girl.

[11] Piaget, *Play, Dreams* and *Imitation*, Chap. 7, especially pp. 179f.
[12] Empson, p. 270.
[13] See *Hoyle's Games*, rev. by R. F. Foster (New York, 1926), p. 178. The forfeiture rule is sometimes understood, sometimes made explicit, as in this edition.

5. Through the Looking-Glass and What Alice Found There

If in *Wonderland* the game comes tumbling down at Alice's challenge, in *Through the Looking-Glass* she sends it tumbling with her own hand. If in *Wonderland* she gets home free, in *Looking-Glass* she wins for her side. What has Alice learned?

As she begins her second adventures her canniness about play and games is not so advanced as that she was waking up to in the first novel. Though half a year older, Alice does not appear to have remembered to be half a year wiser. She still exhibits the eagerness to play the games offered that she did when she first chased after the White Rabbit. Still, by the end, Alice has moved up on a discovery of what it might mean to be one's own grand master.

At the start we find her abandoning her work to play with the black kitten and to teach her chess. She is as fond as ever of "talking to herself" like two people arguing. She not only converses with her kitten but disputes with her. (The narrative itself opens in a disputatious vein.) Alice's idea of play, even of the "let's pretend" type, tends to be social and aggressive. She once startled her nurse with an obvious bit of incorporative wish fulfillment: " 'Nurse! Do let's pretend that I'm a hungry hyaena, and you're a bone!' " (*L-G*, pp. 175–180).

Children like to eat and be merry but often find themselves made to go hungry. Alice is no less concerned with the authoritarian "they" of a little girl's world than if she had never learned to stand up to and throw over authority in Wonderland. She imagines "them" saving up her punishments for her and administering them at a stretch, so that she would have to go without fifty dinners in a row (*L-G*, pp. 178–179). She is eager to escape these authorities by transferring to the Looking-Glass room, where no one will scold her away from the fire. And as from the bottom of the rabbit hole, she imagines being able to taunt those who know she is there but can't get at her (*L-G*, p. 185).

All the same, Alice is not a rebel; she counts on succeeding without insurgency. It is fitting that the poem she encounters in Chapter I, "Jabberwocky," should be concerned with battle, beheading, a victory for the child, and a reward of praise from a parental authority figure. These are the victories and rewards that play can yield a child. Alice hates to be defeated. She doesn't like to confess even to herself that she fails to understand "Jabberwocky," that she can't break its system. She insists that she gets the main point, which is that *"somebody killed something"* (*L-G*, pp. 191f, 197).

Even though Alice's purpose in passing through the glass is to escape the overconstriction of her room at home, which has put her in her original position of "working" at winding a ball of worsted, and which makes no allowance for an untidy "game of romps" between kitten and yarn, we must remember that she herself reprimands (while also kissing) the kitten for its "wicked" gambols (*L-G*, pp. 181, 184, 176). She quite enjoys scolding the kitten as it seems she well knows how, often having been at the receiving end of a scold herself (*L-G*, p. 178). And we should not be surprised that the untidiness of the Looking-Glass room bothers Alices besides intriguing her. She dusts off the White King, who is covered with ashes, and she smooths his hair. She is "anxious to be of use," afraid of frightening the chesspieces, very gentle in lifting the White King after having created the impression of a volcano upon his

Queen by picking her up too suddenly; she is alarmed at alarming the King, concerned about his state (*£-G*, pp. 186–189). Alice remains in many ways a good little girl, carrying over the Looking-Glass threshold precisely the solicitudes and decorums of the authorities she is leaving behind. Yet she is much larger than the chesspieces and can afford to treat them without fear, condescendingly (as she had treated her kittens). So she calls the White King "my dear" and laughs at him. On a sudden whim she guides his pencil as he writes a memorandum, literally overpowering him (*£-G*, pp. 189–190). At this point she is a powerful figure in relation to mere chessmen, who, though alive, stand in relation to her as of children to an adult. In this alien world Alice soon discovers, however, that it is she who is in the position of weakness,[1] no longer the manipulator and controller of chessmen, but one of them. Nor is she in her single self multiple kings and queens as she used to pretend with her sister at home (*£-G*, p. 180); now she is the weakest man, an object to be manipulated and controlled by a power more remote than the "they" she has always known and, what is more, to be domineered over by the other pieces on the board.

The first creatures who put Alice in her place are the Live Flowers she meets in the provoking Looking-Glass garden.[2]

---

[1] See Gardner, ed., *The Annotated Alice*, n. 10, p. 190. Since "Jabberwocky" appears in reverse to Alice, she herself has apparently not been reversed by passing through the mirror. This world is backward to her.

[2] The Live-Flower episode follows Alice's attempts to get to the hill. Her lack of success has been theoretically explained by Clement V. Durrell, "The Theory of Relativity," in *The World of Mathematics*, ed. Newman, II, 1107–1143. Assuming that she is a reflection in a convex mirror, Durrell shows that Alice becomes constantly shorter, as well as thinner. Thus her feet and head don't trace two parallel lines, which would constitute a track along which she could proceed to infinity (as we would normally expect), hence eventually arriving at the hill. Rather her path would end at a point before her projected arrival, where, in fact, she must go out like a candle. Of course, because everything about her would be shrinking proportion-

They are belligerently competitive in their conversation with her: " 'We *can* talk . . . as well as *you* can,' " and so on. Alice is "timid" before them, and allows them to insult her. Although she threatens to pick the Daisies, she does so only out of policy in currying favor with the dominant Tiger-Lily, whom she hopes also to coax into a better temper by compliment. Alice is pleased to listen docilely and to have things explained to her (*L-G*, pp. 200–203).

She is also compliant when she meets the Red Queen, who is now taller than herself and certainly not to be laughed at or condescended to. It is now the Queen who pats Alice on the head like a child. Although at first the Red Queen's advice to walk backward in order to arrive anywhere sounds "nonsense" to Alice, she keeps this to herself, and when she finds the method works, no wonder she is "in awe" of the Red Queen. She even considers trying out the Queen's rules at home, for example, the rule for curtseying to save time while thinking what to say (*L-G*, pp. 205–206).

Alice is willing to accept the fact that she cannot have lost "her way" as all ways here belong to the Red Queen. Alice is "surprised into contradicting her [the Queen] at last" with a "Nonsense," but she immediately fears she may offend the Queen and makes sure to soothe her by curtseying (*L-G*, pp. 206–207).

Alice has been found wanting when asked to answer two key questions: where she is from, and where she is going (*L-G*, p. 206). She is, as in Wonderland, without a clear direction, and happy to find one. Direction is provided much earlier in the book and much more clearly than ever in Wonderland. Again, direction takes the form of a game, whose structure includes a goal for Alice to aim at. The Red Queen is more willing, say, than the Cheshire Cat to tell Alice what to

---

ately, Alice would not notice her own change of size; see especially p. 1113. Though interesting, this theory does not seem to explain why Alice keeps finding herself back at the house.

do and where to go. As it turns out, her advice is misleading, for analysis of the game, whose individual moves are outlined in "The Author's Preface" (*L-G*, p. 172), suggests that the Queening-of-the-Pawn strategy upon which she launches Alice is to the disadvantage of White and Alice, and to the advantage of Red and herself. In accepting this strategy Alice is acting on incomplete information and in ignorance of her opponent's "utilities." She can't act rationally because she doesn't know how the game stands.[3]

From her prospect at the top of the hill (at last) Alice is very excited to see that the whole world is a giant chessboard, and to be able to preview her own future track. Chance is not involved in chess, as it is in cards, so that Alice's adventures through the Looking-Glass have a more predetermined cast than those she had in Wonderland. "For some minutes Alice stood without speaking, looking out in all directions over the country—and a most curious country it was. . . . 'I declare it's marked out just like a large chess-board!' Alice said at last. 'There ought to be some men moving about somewhere—and so there are!' she added in a tone of delight, and her heart began to beat quick with excitement as she went on. 'It's a great huge game of chess that's being played—all over the world— if this *is* the world at all, you know' " (*L-G*, pp. 207–208).

She is to take the place of the White Queen's daughter Lily, who is "too young to play." But in accepting the lowly position of a Pawn, Alice aspires eventually to be a Queen. " 'Oh,

---

[3] The Pawn-to-Queen strategy was apparently a popular one. It is stressed in *Hoyle* (1857), eg., pp. 215f. However, as Gardner points out at length (*The Annotated Alice*, n. 1, p. 170), this is not the strategy which would "maximize" Alice's "utility." Red could be more efficiently checkmated in three moves. The Red Queen is apparently misleading Alice. Alice cannot act "rationally" because she does not have enough information concerning the progress of the game to this point to know what a rational strategy would be.

what fun it is! How I *wish* I was one of them! I wouldn't
mind being a Pawn, if only I might join—though of course I
should *like* to be Queen best' " (*L-G*, p. 208). It is no wonder
that for a little girl the dominant figures should appear as
powerful women, like the chess Queens (or the Queen of
Hearts), and that she should set her hopes on becoming one
of them. For as the Red Queen assures Alice, being Queens
together equals gratification in the form of "feasting and fun."
Alice trusts the Queen's word that she has only to persevere
in passing the eight squares laid out before her, to follow the
rules, and to remember who she is (*L-G*, p. 212).

But of course these are not easy accomplishments in Looking-Glass land. Alice's first movement after her induction into
the game consists of running and getting nowhere (a circumstance perhaps reminiscent of the caucus-race and the illusive-
ness of linear "progress" in games). Alice fails even to succeed
in abiding by the simple rules of conversation that the Red
Queen has just been instructing her in (*L-G*, p. 212). She is
left sparsely enough provided with rules when the Queen suddenly vanishes. Remembering who she is—a matter of keeping terms straight—is to prove equally difficult.

It turns out that Alice is sent through the Third Square
rather than going on her own. The passengers on the train
discuss how she is to be sent, as luggage, parcel post, telegraph,
while Alice insists that she doesn't belong on the journey at
all (*L-G*, p. 219). She does not meet the Man in White Paper's
criterion, that she ought to know where she's going, even if
she doesn't know her name. Still, she duly crosses the bound-
ary of the Fourth Square in spite of all the rules, instructions,
and advice she has received from the passengers, and in spite
of her own disinclination to ride the train at all. That she is on
a determined track is suggested also by her later encounter
with the double finger post:

"TO TWEEDLEDUM'S HOUSE,
"TO THE HOUSE OF TWEEDLEDEE."

These incline Alice to believe that she has choice in determining her path. " 'I'll settle it,' Alice said to herself, 'when the road divides and they point different ways.' " But the road doesn't divide; there is but one road, and it leads to a single place (*L-G*, pp. 227–228). Her apparent freedom to choose her own route is an illusion.

In the Fourth Square Alice's problem is with names as much as with knowing where she is going. The importance of names to the functioning of a system of relationships is made evident. In the nameless woods Alice and the Fawn are companions. Tenniel's illustration shows Alice strolling along with her arm about the Fawn's neck. But when they emerge and the Fawn remembers that Alice is "a human child," it remembers also the attributes which attend this label and dictate rules of relationship, that is, that human beings are to be feared and that a Fawn should run away from a child (*L-G*, pp. 226–227).

The novel presents many instances of concern with definition. There is Alice's confusion concerning whether Humpty-Dumpty wears a cravat or a belt, as she cannot tell its relationship to his body, whether neck or waist (*L-G*, p. 266). There is Humpty-Dumpty's complaint that he cannot distinguish Alice's face from any other human's through lack of what might be called a phonemic principle in the distribution of features (*L-G*, p. 276). And there is the Unicorn's equation, child = fabulous monster. It is important to notice that definition is basically a matter of social agreement. Alice and the Unicorn achieve a good working (or playing) relationship, though they call each other fabulous monsters: " 'If you'll believe in me, I'll believe in you. Is that a bargain?' " (*L-G*, p. 287).

The Gnat had reminded Alice of the advantages of namelessness for allowing one to drop out of an undesirable social system; for example, if she had no name at home, she couldn't be called to lessons (*L-G*, p. 224). Alice, however, prefers definition to loss of identity, even with the unpleasant, sometimes bitter rules that go with it. She is near tears at losing the Fawn, but at the same time she is comforted at finding her own name again (*L-G*, p. 227).

In Chaper IV there is a dance, reminiscent in its peculiar effects of the dance of the Gryphon and the Mock Turtle in Wonderland. Alice suddenly finds herself dancing "in a ring" with the symmetrical pair, Dee and Dum, music playing, and herself singing. " 'I don't know when I began it, but somehow I felt as if I'd been singing it a long long time!' " (*L-G*, p. 232). A dance has a timeless quality (because circular, infinite); but even though it creates the impression that it might just as well go on indefinitely, it still exists in time, and so requires a rule for stopping. " 'Four times round is enough for one dance,' " says Tweedledee (*L-G*, p. 230).

Some such completely arbitrary cutting-off point is customary in a dance, but is less so in a battle, where one expects that the particular moves can only lead to one predictable and inevitable conclusion, one rationally determined by a train of events regulated by clear rules. But in the battle of Tweedledee and Tweedledum the finish is as arbitrary as the beginning (they are fighting over a spoiled rattle, the merest pretext); says Tweedledum, " 'Let's fight till six, and then have dinner!' " (*L-G*, p. 243).

Theirs resembles the battle of the Lion and the Unicorn, members of the military train (all the [White] King's horses and men) that enters the scene after the fall of Humpty-Dumpty. The Lion and the Unicorn are inspired to fight by the convention of a nursery rhyme. They fight in perpetuity. Each has been down some eighty-seven times in the one round (*L-G*, p. 284). As they never get anywhere, their actions could be conceived as a form of dance. Neither ever actually wins the crown, and they stop only for refreshments—white bread, brown bread, and plumcake. It is not even certain who has had the best of it in the current bout; in fact, the Unicorn phrases his victory statement as a question (*L-G*, p. 286). Apparently, the White King considers the battle a joke, for he is in no real fear of loosing his crown (*L-G*, p. 283). The only end consists in both contestants' being drummed out of town, frustrated of their feast (*L-G*, pp. 284–291). These two battles are extraordinary because while they purport to be competitive structures no rules exist for deciding between the two competitors, so that their movements fall into a circular ritual pattern leading to no necessary end at all; it merely stops, like a dance.

But the frustrating peculiarity of Looking-Glass games does not prevent them from being a way of life, so that a great many activities are spoken of as if they were games with rules. The poor untidy and pin-pricked White Queen is sorry she can't remember the "rule" for being glad. She assumes that if Alice knew this rule, happiness would be available to her whenever she liked. It's a matter of will; just as one may remedy tears by choosing to "consider," so may one believe things by trying (*L-G*, pp. 250–251).

Though the White Queen attributes so much to Alice's powers of will at this point, significantly she suggests for Alice —who has retrieved the brush from its entanglement in the bedraggled Queen's hair and set her uncooperative shawl straight—the position of lady's maid. Alice is still hoping to learn other people's game systems and is willing to bend her will to them. All she asks is to be instructed. Of course she does not favor the position of maid, any more than she liked being mistaken for Mary Ann by the White Rabbit. By the same token, after the White Queen's squeaks modulate into the bleats of the Sheep, Alice can put up with only so much of her pronounced unsheepishness. She finally becomes "rather vexed" with the Sheep for ordering her about by the terms and rules of rowing, which are so much gibberish to Alice. She is offended at being called a "little goose." But the Sheep refuses to instruct Alice and only laughs scornfully at her misunderstanding. At the same time the Sheep disavows any authority over Alice (such as would be implied by teaching her the game). When Alice pleads for the Sheep to stop the boat so as to get to the beautiful rushes, the Sheep answers, "How am I to stop it? . . . If you leave off rowing, it'll stop of itself' " (*L-G*, pp. 255, 259). In the Sheep resides something of the perversity of the Cheshire Cat, that is, in the refusal to tell Alice what to do, or to do it for her. The Sheep won't even tell her what game is being played. Alice is forced to learn to do for herself.

Humpty-Dumpty, incarnation of the elusive egg in the Sheep's Shop, has plenty of will. Alice notices that Humpty-Dumpty talks about conversation " 'just as if it was a game' " (*L-G*, p. 265). (We may compare the conversation between Alice and the White King, which takes the form of an actual parlor game—" 'I love my love with an H,' " etc.) (*L-G*, p. 279). Humpty-Dumpty assumes, for instance, that all of Alice's questions are riddles to be triumphantly solved; and he speaks of taking turns in choosing a subject. For Humpty-Dumpty "glory" means a "nice knock-down argument," which of course implies the need for a conversational opponent to knock down (*L-G*, pp. 268–269).

Humpty-Dumpty displays the true game-instituter's attitude about language: " 'When I use a word,' Humpty-Dumpty said in a rather scornful tone, "it means just what I choose it to mean —neither more nor less.' " He simply assumes control over the system; he does not let conventions rule him but makes his own. " 'The question is,' said Humpty-Dumpty, 'which is to be master, that's all.' " This remark defines the egocentric aspect of game-playing, their creation by fiat. But Alice questions Humpty-Dumpty on the social aspect, " 'whether you *can* make words mean so many different things.' " This amounts to asking whether words work (for communication) if they are so purely private. Humpty-Dumpty, however, is not at all unwilling to institute his private language as a social one. He is "very much pleased" when Alice asks him to explain his term "Impenetrability": " 'Now you talk like a reasonable child,' said Humpty-Dumpty." More than anyone else Humpty-Dumpty provides Alice with an example of how one may create one's own games by fiat and then induce and instruct others to play them (*L-G*, p. 269).

In this he differs from the Sheep, who scorns to let Alice in on her game. Humpty-Dumpty likes nothing better than to do so. He is all eagerness to explain "Jabberwocky" to Alice, and Alice is very willing to follow his lead, for instance divining the meaning of "wabe" according to this system. She is "surprised at her own ingenuity"; she still likes to enjoy her cleverness in mastering somebody else's game. But of course she eventually finds Humpty-Dumpty a bit overbearing. Although he has allowed Alice in on his language, he always reserves the right to pull the carpet out from under her. Characteristically, he ends their encounter at his own will, without reference to hers: " 'That's all . . . Good-by' " (*L-G*, pp. 272–276).

Alice has found some encouragement in her hopes of understanding the systems of conventions by which Looking-Glass creatures operate. And there are all sorts of systems going around and around outside the chess game. This is indicated, for example, by the White King's comment that while two of his horses, the two Knights, are occupied in the chess game, the other four thousand two hundred and seven are available for other activities (*L-G*, pp. 278–279).

When the horsemen surround her in the forest of the Seventh Square, Alice thinks she observes a "regular rule" dictating that whenever a soldier's horse stumbles, the rider must instantly fall off (*L-G*, p. 277). She is encouraged to think in these terms all the more because the inhabitants of Looking-Glass land consciously follow formal rules in their behavior; this makes their actions appear predetermined, like those of puppets. For example, in their struggle to ascertain whether Alice must fall prisoner to the Red Knight, or whether the White Knight has truly delivered her, the two Knights agree to fight by the "Rules of Battle." Alice is interested to decipher the rules from the behavior: " 'I wonder, now, what the Rules of Battle are,' she said to herself, as she watched the fight, timidly peeping out from her hiding-place. 'One Rule seems to be, that if one Knight hits the other, he knocks him off his horse; and, if he misses, he tumbles off himself—and another Rule seems to be that they hold their clubs with their arms, as if they were Punch and Judy—' " (*L-G*, p. 295). And the narrator remarks, "Another Rule of Battle, that Alice had not noticed, seemed to be that they always fell on their heads; and the battle ended with their both falling off in this way, side by side" (*L-G*, p. 296). The rules of battle never come altogether clear to Alice, and she cannot tell whether or not it was a "glorious victory" as the White Knight claims. Besides, as Alice says, " 'I don't want to be anybody's prisoner. I want to be a Queen!' " (*L-G*, p. 296).

The White Knight is an entirely mental being, who sings a song featuring a dreamer of futile masterpieces who resembles himself. The Knight's mind keeps on "working" no matter where his body, even if it be upside down. His mind works on purportedly useful inventions, all of which are quite useless. A typical example is the pudding that the Knight feels was clever to invent, but as he also sadly confesses, never was and never will be cooked; it is a medley of inedible ingredients (*L-G*, pp. 297–305). The Knight's inventions transcend such utilitarianisms as digestibility anyway.

Alice is taken with the White Knight. And though sometimes tempted to laugh at his horsemanship—she once calls him "ridiculous," observing that he'd do better on a wooden horse with wheels—she doesn't dare because he looks so solemn (*L-G*, p. 301). She is full of solicitude for his many tumbles, and she waits kindly to see him off. The Knight is at liberty only to go as far as his move, no farther (*L-G*, p. 296). In certain respects the game controls the participants and dictates the extent of allowable relationships between them. But, whatever her kindness to the Knight, Alice is not overly reluctant to see him go, nor bitter that the game makes this inevitable. She is very eager " 'for the last brook, and to be a Queen' " (*L-G*, p. 314).

Alice is pleased at becoming a Queen at last, and she expects certain things of herself if she really is a Queen: that now she will be dignified and that she will be able to "manage" the crown. She even supposes that the game might be over, now that she has made it. However, it is not, and as she begins to discover, she has not. She is still "timid," "piteous," with the two other Queens. In spite of the fact that she is a person who is "always ready for a little argument" and that she actually succeeds in talking down one of the Red Queen's rules (on the grounds that if one never spoke until spoken to, the game of conversation could never begin), the Queens still definitely domineer over her. They insist on an examination. When she attempts resistance, the Red Queen squelches it by claiming that she has a nasty, vicious temper, the White Queen asserting that Alice's state is such that she wants to deny something, but doesn't know what. The latter diagnosis is about accurate. Alice is feeling frustrated in finding that, now a Queen, she is apparently as powerless as ever to accomplish anything on her own. She thinks, for example, that she should be the one inviting guests to her own feast; instead, the other two Queens coolly invite each other (*L-G*, pp. 317–320).

Alice thinks to herself, " 'What dreadful nonsense we *are* talking' "—it is still "we" committing the nonsense. She has gone along with the examination. And of course she fails. Alice "turns suddenly" on the White Queen (the less intimidating of the two), declaring that she doesn't like "being found fault with so much." She turns a question around, as she thinks, "triumphantly" upon the Red Queen: " 'If you'll tell me what language 'fiddle-de-dee' is, I'll tell you the French for it!' " However, her triumph is premature. The answer backfires, for the Red Queen gets the last word: " 'Queens never make bargains.' " She and the White Queen are still laying out the grounds, making the rules; they are not stooping to agree on them with Alice. One of the most maddeningly insidious of such rules is one which might well be adapted from chess and applied to conversation: " 'When you've once said a thing, that fixes it, and you must take the consequences.' " A rule like this catches Alice in the nonsense (*L-G*, pp. 321–323).[4]

Alice definitely has not got it made just because she has reached the Eighth Square. Although there is an arch marked "Queen Alice," there is "no admittance" for her, since of the two existing bell pulls one is for visitors, one for servants, and she is neither. Again, she feels that those rights she had expected to assume once a Queen have been outrageously denied her. Alice responds "angrily," and she is "ready to find fault with anybody" (*L-G*, pp. 327–328). In the song which issues when the door is finally flung open, it is still somebody else making invitations to Alice's feast. The song also forecasts an unappetizing, even a spoiled feast, not a bit the "feasting and fun" she had been promised (*L-G*, pp. 329–330).

Once more Alice is intimidated. She glances "nervously" at the table. She even feels glad that someone else has invited the guests, for she reflects that she wouldn't have known whom to ask. She longs for somebody else to speak. She is "anxious" about carving the joint. The Red Queen takes immediate advantage of Alice's timorousness by imperially noting her tardiness—she had missed the first two courses. The Queen has those that follow removed before Alice can eat (*L-G*, pp. 330–331).

[4] Cf. *Hoyle* (1857), pp. 208–209; he defines very strictly the player's commitment to a move once taken, even if by mistake.

This little girl's nightmare of scolding and withholding of food by a representative of the authorities follows Alice's struggle to play the game as a humble, obedient Pawn in the hopes of becoming a Queen. Being Queen does not amount to much. She is not a poor-spirited child, and when she finds herself thus cheated and browbeaten at the moment of expected triumph, she becomes self-righteously indignant: "She didn't see why the Red Queen should be the only one to give orders; so, as an experiment, she called out 'Waiter! Bring back the pudding!' " This very important experiment in will works magically, for "there it was again in a moment, like a conjuring trick" (*L-G*, pp. 331–332).

After her boldness Alice suffers a reaction. She is shy before the pudding, who accuses her of impertinence. She is "very polite" with the White Queen. The Red Queen takes over again, leading the toast while Alice is stuck answering a riddle. The creatures eat like pigs, while at the same time Alice is being scolded for lack of manners. This amounts to a galling invocation of discriminatory rules, as in the Wonderland court scene. And yet Alice is still cowed. Although she tries to decline the Queen's offer of "support," when actually pressed she "tried to submit to it with a good grace." But Alice does not fail to recognize the unhelpful nature of this supposed aid; as she later recalls, in supporting her, " 'they wanted to squeeze me flat!' " (*L-G*, pp. 332–334).

At this point the food takes over the feast, a reversal of the hoped-for "feasting and fun." " 'I can't stand this any longer,' " cries Alice. She is no longer willing to "submit," as the game is denying her all the payoffs that would make it worth her while to play. She turns "fiercely" on the Red Queen, whom she considers the cause of the mischief (*L-G*, p. 336).

This scene differs somewhat from the corresponding disruption scene in the Wonderland card court in that Alice physically executes the disruption herself. She pulls the tablecloth from the table, and with it plates, dishes, guests, and candles.

And she catches hold of the Red Queen (*L-G*, p. 336); in the chess game she has captured the Queen and checkmated the Red King. Whereas Alice abolished her commitment to the game in *Wonderland* by declaring it a mere game, she wins for her side in *Looking-Glass*.[5] There remains no possibility that as upsetter of the game she forfeits it, because she finishes the game before overturning it. She shakes the Red Queen back into a kitten (*L-G*, p. 336). Alice is able to win because she finally quits trying to play the hopelessly muddled and stacked game(s) she finds thrust upon her (though never fully explained to her) in Looking-Glass land. By asserting her own will she at the same time acts in accordance with the rules of actual chess, which are unmuddled, stable, and hence fair enough to make victory possible.

White wins the game through Alice's checkmate. But that is not strictly equivalent to saying that Alice herself wins. We never see who is manipulaing the pieces on this board—unless it is Alice's dreaming consciousness. Or is it the Red King's? The narrator leaves this as a question in Alice's mind and as a question open to the reader at the end (*L-G*, p. 344).

It is possible that the Red King should dream a dream in which he loses. Yet in checkmating the King, may not Alice be fulfilling her intention expressed but not acted upon in Chapter VIII—to wake him just to see what will happen? She wouldn't like " 'belonging to another person's dream' " (*L-G*, p. 293). The situation is of course ambiguous, but it appears that the dream may be Alice's, for she doesn't disappear upon attacking the Red King. It is he who dwindles to a wooden chesspiece. Tweedledum had told Alice that she couldn't wake the King if she tried (*L-G*, p. 239), but she doesn't herself accept this, as she later thinks of trying (*L-G*, p. 293). At any rate,

[5] See Carroll, "The Author's Preface," *The Annotated Alice* ed. Gardner, p. 172; this lists the moves of the game ending with "11. Alice takes the R.Q. and Wins."

whereas at first she had feared the King's waking (*L-G*, p. 239), at the end she has the courage to risk possible annihilation in order to convince herself she is not a figment in another's dream. By the same token she challenges the necessity of being a Pawn in another's game. In an absolute sense, she may indeed exist in a dream, function in a game not her own. But she has done what she can to make both dream and game hers. The question is which is to be master.

6. Sport

Sylvie and Bruno and Sylvie and Bruno Concluded

The White Knight's song supports the virtues of play by undermining those of earnestness and work. Yet Carroll shows in the *Alices* the subversion rather than the fair success of play worlds. This subversion occurs because (1) Carroll conceives play as fundamentally competitive, that is, as games, and (2) games are the products of will. The will which realizes that games are created by its fiat, that considers them forms of aggression, tends to find terms and rules a balking of its own power and of its chances of demolishing the opponent. It tends to find terms and rules dispensable. The egocentric may then overbalance the social aspect of game playing, which is what happens in Wonderland and Looking-Glass land, where Alice is deluded in thinking she is playing bona fide parlor-type games; she is either not let in on the terms and rules, or else they aren't fixed. Most of the time it is a matter of crocodile-eat-fish, of Fury and the Mouse.

The danger involved is clear to see in the croquet match. The Queen is so likely to win, it's hardly worth finishing the game, a way of saying that it's hardly a game at all. For a game supposes a stable structure, one recognized by all players, and one not adjusted constantly at the whim and to the advantage of the strongest player. The match comes close to being what Carroll often termed "sport," whose meaning should become clearer as we look, to begin with, at the *Sylvie and Bruno* books.

i

Sylvie and Bruno and *Sylvie and Bruno Concluded* (1889, 1893) add up to nine hundred odd pages of what Carroll calls in his preface to *Sylvie and Bruno*, "litterature," a peculiar narrative threading of "random flashes of thought" and "dream-suggestions." The "stringing together, upon the thread of a consecutive story" of these materials is most unusual. (It took Carroll some ten years even to classify his odds and ends sufficiently to begin combining them) (I, x).[1] Critics hardly know what to say about the phenomenon these novels present. Perhaps a typical reaction is that of John Francis McDermott, who falls back on what may be termed the schizophrenia theory: the good part of *Sylvie and Bruno* is Carroll, the bad part Dodgson. One of the few to be intrigued rather than put off by the books is Evelyn Waugh, on the grounds that they suggest insights into "one of the great imaginative writers of the language."[2]

The story contained in the two volumes may be recounted with a certain appearance of lucid sequence:

> Our Narrator, a dreamy old man with a propensity for the "eerie" state, wherein he is able to see fairies, traces two simultaneous plot lines, one transpiring in the magic realm of Outland, one in Elveston, England. Sylvie and Bruno are the charming children of the good Warden of

---

[1] *Sylvie and Bruno* and *Sylvie and Bruno Concluded* are hereafter identified in the text as volumes I and II, with page reference.

[2] McDermott, ed., "Introduction," *The Russian Journal*, pp. 32–38; Waugh, "Carroll and Dodgson," *Spectator*, CLXIII (Oct. 13, 1939), 511. Waugh too accepts the split-personality theory but does not discount the *Sylvie and Bruno* novels as the product of the dull Dodgson half; however, he does not actually have much to say on the novels.

Outland, who is embarking upon a journey, occasion for a conspiracy on the part of the Vice-Warden and his lady: they trick him into signing the wrong document, thereby deeding all power to themselves and inheritance to their fat, loveless son Uggug instead of the rightful Bruno. A Beggar comes to the palace. Through the aid of the kindly Professor and the mad Gardener, Sylvie and Bruno follow him, and he proves to be their father, now King of Elfland. He offers Sylvie a choice between two magic lockets, one reading ALL WILL LOVE SYLVIE, the other SYLVIE WILL LOVE ALL. Sylvie chooses the latter. Meanwhile (and this includes much) Sylvie, though only about ten, is very like the grown-up Lady Muriel Orme, whom the Narrator first meets on the train to Elveston, where he is to visit, for health's sake, his old friend Doctor Arthur Forester. Arthur loves Lady Muriel but fears he is too old to win her. Lady Muriel's cousin arrives at Elveston; he, it appears, does have a claim on her hand. By now Sylvie and Bruno have become full fairies by passing through the gates to Elfland. They appear to the Narrator in the Elveston woods. Life-size, they appear at the Evelston station, and Eric saves Bruno from being run over by a train. Sylvie and Bruno are invited to a party by Lady Muriel and her father the Earl, where their magic flowers astonish the guests. Lady Muriel is engaged to Eric, and Arthur resolves to depart for India. However, Eric's lack of religion causes a breakup of the engagement, and, we find out, Lady Muriel never did love him *in that way*. Sylvie and Bruno are in the district and their adventures with the Narrator confirm their character as fairies who do good. For one thing, they steer the shy Arthur to Lady Muriel, who are then duly engaged. They appear again at a party, this time startling the guests with Sylvie's heavenly music. Lady Muriel's friend, Mein Herr, who resembles the Professor, is introduced. News comes of an epidemic at a nearby village. Arthur must go, an hour after he and Lady Muriel are married. News follows of his death. Several months later our Narrator returns to Elveston. The grieving Lady Muriel receives some solace, for Sylvie and Bruno appear to her as well as the Narrator, singing their unearthly theme song, "I'm sure it is nothing but Love." This is their last appearance among human beings, for they return to Outland for the Professor's long-awaited Lecture and the Banquet. However, a hurricane and the arrival of the Beggar (Elf King) disrupt the feast. The Vice-Warden and his lady repent and are forgiven. But loveless Uggug is transformed into a furious Porcupine. The Narrator sees Sylvie and Bruno in a last vision after it has been discovered that Arthur is alive, that Eric saved him from the village, afterward receiving inklings of religion, and that the devoted Lady Muriel will now nurse her husband back to health. The novel closes with the revelation that the double magic lockets are really one and with the angel voice of Sylvie whispering, "It is Love."

ii

Probably most people having read the two books but not having taken notes could not reconstruct even this sketchy a sequence. As Carroll says in the preface to *Sylvie and Bruno* concerning mnemonic aids, "memory needs *links*" (I, xiv), and the *Sylvie and Bruno* books hang together (if they do at all) by very tenuous narrative links. To accept these novels, I believe the reader's state must be as incapable of rufflement as the Narrator's, who says at yet another eerie seizure and the appearance of fairies in the drawing room, " 'I felt no shock of surprise, but accepted the fact with the same unreasoning apathy with which one meets the events of a dream.' " (II, 152).

The dream aspect of the narrative works two ways. As is

the usual case, waking life influences the dream experience. For example, the dropping of a poker by the Narrator—he has fallen asleep gazing at the fire—is transformed in his fairy dream into the explosive experiment that concludes the Professor's Lecture (II, 344–345). But influence operates the other way too. What happens in the dream infiltrates reality. So upon first encountering Lady Muriel, the Narrator imagines away her veil and sees the face of Sylvie (I, 17–18). This fantasy turns out to be true to life. And, to give another example, the badinage of Lady Muriel and Arthur recapitulates the tone and style of Sylvie and Bruno (II, 118).

This two-way permeability gives dream and reality, Elfland and Elveston, equal or equally questionable status: " 'So, either I've been dreaming about Sylvie,' I said to myself, 'and this is the reality. Or else I've really been with Sylvie, and this is a dream! Is Life itself a dream, I wonder?' " (I, 19).

The Narrator is inclined in the Sylvie and Bruno books much more than in the Alices to direct philosophizing of this sort (through the sentiment itself might suit either) because the later work is a "new departure" and intended to mix "some of the graver thoughts of human life" with "acceptable nonsense for children" (I, xvi), an often incongruous and sometimes irritating mixture. Indeed, the nonsense itself sometimes fails to be entirely acceptable. Sometimes the wordplay has the spare, dry, not to say grim, humor of the Alices—as when Bruno, having enjoyed a piece of cake, is horrified at being asked whether he has enjoyed himself (II, 374–375). But too often humor turns to cuteness as the jokes are hint-hintingly explained: Uggug has been dragged from the room by the ear, and his mother says to the Lord Chancellor, " 'Your Lordship has a very taking way with children! I doubt if any one could gain the ear of my darling Uggug so quickly as you can!' For an entirely stupid woman, my Lady's remarks were curiously full of meaning, of which she herself was wholly unconscious" (I, 44).

Another version of the interinfluence of dream and reality appears in the Narrator's tendency to assert the interinfluence of literature and reality. Of course the usual direction of flow is reality→literature. But on occasion the Narrator reverses this such that his literary imaginings come first and actual fact follows after. The Narrator makes things up in words as well as dreams, as when he meets the veiled Lady Muriel on the train: " 'The lady had a perfectly formed nose,' I caught myself saying to myself, 'hazel eyes, and lips—' and here it occurred to me that to see, for myself, what 'the lady' was really like, would be more satisfactory than much speculation."

Peculiar about this passage is the Narrator's use of the past tense—" 'The lady *had* a perfectly formed nose,' " and so on, for this indicates that he conceives his adventure as a fait accompli, a closed book, here at the outset of a narrative yet to be unfolded. In fact, the Narrator appears to be highly self-conscious that the whole affair follows the lines of a novel: " 'And this is, of course, the opening scene of Vol I. *She* is the heroine. And *I* am one of those subordinate characters that only turn up when needed for the development of her destiny, and whose final appearance is outside the church, waiting to greet the Happy Pair!' " (I, 17–18).

This double narrative, with its double permeability, is often more memorable for the strain and oddness of its links than for the successful threading of a consecutive story. The first volume begins with the words "—and then" (I, 1), and just as Carroll says his ideas came to him like "an effect without a cause" (I, x), so do many incidents in the *Sylvie and Bruno* books follow one on another. Often the novels resemble in their narrative structure, or nonstructure, the stories told by Bruno, who adores a wild assortment of dramatis personae more than he cares for cause/effect plot logic. Here is an extract:

"Once there were a Mouse and a Crocodile and a Man

and a Goat and a Lion. . . . And the Mouse found a
Shoe, and it thought it were a Mouse-trap. So it got
right in, and it stayed ever so long." "Why did it *stay*
in?" said Sylvie. . . . " 'Cause it thought it couldn't get
out again," Bruno explained. . . . "But why did it go in
at all?" said Sylvie. "—and it jamp and jamp," Bruno pro-
ceeded, ignoring this question, "and at last it got right
out again. And it looked at the mark in the Shoe. And the
Man's name were in it. So it knew it wasn't its own
Shoe." [I, 375–376]

One can hardly recall the Mouse or the Shoe or why they
were part of the story by the time one has arrived at the end.

Carroll's conjunctions are not all so primitive as Bruno's
"and's" and "so's," though they are often as gratuitous and
disorienting. He employs a variety of means of bridging between the disparate worlds experienced by the Narrator.

The asleep-over-the-fire-dreaming-an-adventure kind of
bridge is relatively conventional and cumbersome. Carroll sets
out to be original, and he is, often accomplishing a quicker
and more "eerie" transition by a word, a phrase. For example,
the unlovely Vice-Warden's wife is referred to as "my Lady."
The Professor is guiding her in to her Outlandish breakfast.
"And then with (as it seemed to me) most superfluous politeness, he flung open the door to my compartment, and ushered
in—'a young and lovely lady!' I muttered to myself with some
bitterness" (I, 16). With this mid-sentence transformation of
context we are with Lady Muriel on the train. Later in the
chapter Lady Muriel is as abruptly replaced by my Lady. One
moment the Narrator is discussing literature with Lady Muriel,
who says we will eventually see it reduced, as by the Rule of
Least Common Multiple, if we only wait, and then without
warning my Lady is telling Uggug " 'there's no use waiting' "
—for something else entirely of course, but the desired transfer from this world to that has been accomplished (I, 23).

Sometimes the Narrator's own words go out of control, as when he begins musing to himself on his dream, " 'I thought I saw . . . ,' " and the phrase commences to conjugate itself, finally going off into Outland and the Gardener's song:

> "He thought he saw an Elephant
> That practiced on a fife:
> He looked again, and found it was
> A letter from his wife.
> 'At length I realize,' he said,
> 'The bitterness of Life!' "   [I, 65]

The mad Gardner sings many stanzas of this song at intervals (frequently transitional) throughout both books. Each stanza recapitulates this pattern: he thought he saw a —— but looked again and found it was a ——. This could also be taken for a pattern in the Narrator's own apprehension of things, for as described in the *Alices* or graphically presented in the *Wonderland Postage-Stamp Case,* manifold transformations occur in *Sylvie and Bruno* and *Sylvie and Bruno Concluded.* The Narrator can never be sure where he is or whom he's dealing with—like the Professor, who, when waked up demands courteously to know, " 'whereabouts we are just now—and *who* we are, beginning with me?' " (I, 263).

There are a series of suggested doubles in the novels. Strongly suggested are Sylvie and Bruno/Lady Muriel and Arthur, but as we've seen, that doesn't preclude a passing connection between Lady Muriel and the Vice-Wardeness, transitionally convenient, though thematically meaningless since Lady Muriel is the perfection of young ladyhood and the Vice-Wardeness is a fat conspirator upon whose broad face a dim-witted smile is lost like a lone ripple and whose hands, when clapped, resound like the percussion of featherbeds. Also a merely incidental or convenient link connects Bruno to the Earl, than whom no two characters could be less alike, one "an embodied Mischief" (II, 250), who talks meant-to-be-

lovable baby talk, the other a philosophical-minded old gentleman; nevertheless the Earl uncannily echoes certain of
Bruno's words (I, 246).

It may be imagined how confusing these whimsical dou-
blings can become. A more likely pair is that of the Professor/
Narrator. Both are eccentrically learned types, both vaguely
established as objects of pity due to illness, both friends to
Sylvie and Bruno; and besides, the Professor's words upon
waking, as quoted above, follow the Narrator's falling asleep
(I, 263). A character can have multiple doubles; the Professor
has another. The human but mysterious friend of Lady Muriel
is at once Mein Herr and the Professor; says the Narrator,
"The figure outside seemed to be changing at every moment,
like one of the shapes in a kaleidoscope" (II, 98).

Kaleidoscopic well describes the narrative patterns in the
Sylvie and Bruno books in spite of the fixed outlines of the
main plots: Sylvie and Bruno join their father in Elfland after
the foul conspiracy has been scotched; Arthur and Muriel,
difficulties of a rival claim and mortal danger surmounted,
are married and live happily ever after. As for an all-informing
moral idea in this shifting picture, we might say with Sylvie
after acting audience to Bruno, " 'The Story's finished! And
whatever is to be *learned* from it,' she added, aside to me, 'I'm
sure I don't know!' " (I, 382). This assessment is apt even
though the *Sylvie and Bruno* books end with a clear moral
announcement about love.

The reason is that the perplexities of the form of the novels
probably impress us more than what is extractably clear in
plot and theme. Much of the pleasure to be had in reading
these books comes from putting together the pieces, or more
accurately, from enjoying Carroll's cleverly unlikely conjunctions and the dissolves which open the way for further surprises. The *Sylvie and Bruno* novels are meant to amuse. They
contain an element of play resembling the puzzle games of *A
Tangled Tale*, for in both prefaces Carroll sets the reader

something to guess: "My readers may perhaps like to amuse themselves by trying to detect, in a given passage, the one piece of 'padding' it contains (I, xi–xii). On occasion he interrupts his narrative with an appeal to the readers to help him unravel a puzzle (I, 228). Presumably he amuses himself in relating the story, for he tells us that writing his books is not at all a matter of fulfilling a "task," of producing a "tale of bricks" like a slave. Carroll's writing is not work, and if it were, he suggests, it would be work to read. There must be free, self-motivating desire (recalling Schiller's comparison of play and art). The writing can be called a task only in the sense of "the task I have set myself" (I, xi–xii; see also II, xi, xvii).

iii

We may not be entirely happy that Carroll chose to mix with his kaleidoscopically playful nonsense "thoughts. . . not wholly out of harmony with the graver cadences of Life" (I, xiii), although we surely must concede that it *was* a new departure. Since I don't think that these graver thoughts, which are most interesting in themselves, really coalesce with the nonsense (except in the general sense that it is playful and some of the thoughts are on play) such that form and content must by rights be treated as one thing, I will consider now in semi-isolation the main theme in these books as it relates in particular to play, games, and sport. In both prefaces Carroll discusses the last of this trio and defends the fact that in *Sylvie and Bruno* and *Sylvie and Bruno Concluded* "I should have treated with such entire want of sympathy the British passion for 'Sport' " (I, xx).

But let us take play and games first. The *Sylvie and Bruno* books have something to say about the theoretical query, how does one pass the time, or what is pastime? Carroll presents two choices: (1) ecstatic bliss or nirvana, which makes time and consciousness cease to exist, or else (2) striving toward some self-proposed end, which gives time and consciousness a purpose and makes them pleasant. Carroll offers music and dance as emblems of the nirvana solution, but the solution he really backs appears to be diversions in time, an infinite stretch of them. Diversions of this sort, including all games, are characterized by highly defined time limits and goal orientation. Passages in *Sylvie and Bruno* and *Sylvie and Bruno Concluded* and their prefaces, which offer observations on a variety of subjects Carroll considered important, circle intriguingly around these characteristics and the problems that go with them.

As part of a moral disquisition on preparing for death inserted into the preface of *Sylvie and Bruno*, the unsettling specter is raised of a perpetual existence beyond the grave, more terrible than simple annihilation: "endless ages . . . , with nothing to do, nothing to hope for, nothing to love!" (I, xvii). The same idea appears later in a conversation between Arthur and Lady Muriel, where it is remarked about a projected infinite expanse of future history, " 'The day must come—if the world lasts long enough . . . when every possible tune will have been composed—every possible pun perpetrated . . . and worse than that, every possible *book* written! For the number of *words* is finite' " (II, 131). (The problem raised is as disconcerting as that threatened by the game theorists, who will no doubt someday break chess, as people have already broken tic-tac-toe and other closed systems.)

The prospect of infinity is evoked again in a speech by the old Earl in *Sylvie and Bruno Concluded*. He is disturbed by the "nightmare" that in eternity men would run out of activities to occupy their minds. This would most obviously occur in practical fields like medicine, but could happen also in the theoretical field of mathematics: " 'Surely the time, needed to exhaust *all* the novelty and interest of the subject, would be absolutely *finite*? And so of all other branches of Science.' " " 'With nothing more to learn, can one rest content on *knowl-*

edge, for the eternity yet to be lived through?' " No help out of this dilemma is to be had by proposing work for others as a filler of eternity. " 'Yes,' said the Earl, 'so long as there *were* any others needing help. But, given ages and ages more, surely all created reasons would at length reach the same dead level of *satiety.* And *then* what is there to look forward to?' " (II, 255–260).

The bind is that people require always something "to look forward to"; a goal confers value upon our activity. "Intensity of thought," mastering a subject, are the secrets of enjoying life—"like a hungry man sitting down to dinner" (I, 335–336). But once the goal is reached, it is without value. "Satiety" is the opposite of intensity and hunger. It is very well to live by a sort of Browningesque aspiration theory one's life through, but through eternity?[3]

[3] Alain Robbe-Grillet has compared Carroll's work with Beckett's *Waiting for Godot* in that each presents a world where essentially time does not pass (there is a perpetual present, as in eternity). And yet time is felt heavily as moment following moment, and the characters long for it to lead somewhere (as in a game). An analogy might be drawn between the hoped-for arrival of Godot and winning once and for all, impossibilities in such temporal eternities, unless time itself could be stopped. What remains in Carroll's and Beckett's worlds, according to Robbe-Grillet, is a realization that the human condition is "to be there," from the horrible satiety of which, it should be added, men partially save themselves by projecting a series of elsewheres toward which they may strive. See Robbe-Grillet, "Samuel Beckett, Or Presence on the Stage," in *For a New Novel: Essays on Fiction*, trans. Richard Howard (New York, 1965), pp. 119, 111. The best analysis I know of this paradox of diversion is Pascal's (his examples, gambling, games, hunting, and other pleasure-seeking) : diversion is pointless from a practical standpoint, but undertaken to divert one from the unbearable condition of just being there with oneself. It sets itself time limits and goals. The anticipated pleasure of reaching the goal evaporates upon achievement. And time stretches out again, only to be passed by the provision of another goal. See Blaise Pascal, *Pensées,* trans. with introd. Martin Turnell (New York, 1962), nos. 265, 267, 269, 275, 276, pp. 174–182.

Carroll's Earl allows himself sometimes to evade the prospect of an eventual running out of things toward which to aspire, and worse, a running out of the energy of aspiration. He is sometimes tempted to pray for personal annihilation, or a type of Buddhist nirvana (II, 259).

On several occasions Carroll offers images of something not unlike a timeless, self-sufficient, nonstriving nirvana. One of these depends on a narrow confinement of time (one hour). This eliminates the necessity of consciousness of sequence, so that the experience may be imagined as an undivided moment of ecstasy. In a burst of enthusiasm about the essence of life and the possibility that it may exist in spirits that men do not perceive, the Narrator asks, "Did not God make this swarm of happy insects, to dance in the sunbeam for one hour of bliss, for no other object, that we can imagine, than to swell the sum of conscious happiness?" (II, 302). Here is continuous fulfillment without desire, for the insects entertain no object in the normal sense of the word; the only object is God's, and that of course is beyond understanding in the normal sense too.

The insects are said to "dance."[4] Another activity that approaches the condition of pure goalless process is music. Both embody essential play impulses, being self-motivating, self-gratifying, nonutilitarian, and circular activities. Much is made, especially in *Sylvie and Bruno Concluded*, of Sylvie's musical ability. The ineffable air she plays at Lady Muriel's party produces the common signs of ecstasy: a "rapt expression" on Sylvie's face, and "pure joy" attended by thrilling of the hearts of the audience (II, 177–178). Her voice has a yet more magical impact in the novel's theme song, "I'm sure it is nothing but Love." It produces in the Narrator a "sharp pang"; it pierces his heart. The experience is compared to the in-

---

[4] Sewell (*The Field of Nonsense*, pp. 190–191) describes dancing as an ultimate mystic game—as doing not making—and points out the dearth of dancing except in grotesque forms in Carroll's writing.

stantaneous seeing and realizing of one's "idea of perfect beauty" (II, 306–307). The effect combines a weeping of "pure delight" and a sort of divine terror. There is no question of either aspiration or satiety at such a moment. This kind of ecstatic nirvana, however, is not the solution proposed by Arthur in responding to the Earl's dilemma about eternity. (We should remember that Alice cannot sustain a timeless, motiveless consciousness; she becomes restless with the various songs and dances and can't help hoping to get on with it—the game.)[5] Arthur's solution simply promises that while individual games are finite, there is an infinite number of games, most not yet imagined, to fill eternity.

He uses the analogy of a child playing with his toys. The child might reason that in thirty years' time " 'I shall have had enough of bricks and ninepins. How weary Life will be!' " Yet after thirty years the man will be engaged in new occupations quite inconceivable to the child-mind (II, 260). By implication, the man is but playing with new toys. Arthur projects the same relationship between the games of the man's life and those stretching out forever in the afterlife. His heaven is one of infinite temporal sequence, a linear conception. The essential requirement is that interest not flag, that a man be able perpetually to propose to himself new games. And this is provided for in the *Sylvie and Bruno* books by Arthur's repeated emphasis on the unfailing energy of Free Will (e.g., I, 390–391, II, 122–123). Free Will is outside the rules of any system. It is what institutes systems.

In both novels Carroll is committed to an ideal of playfulness. The notion of the innocence of play is perhaps most directly expressed in a moralizing episode in *Sylvie and Bruno*

[5] Carroll certainly recognized the difficulty of sustaining conscious happiness. As Miss H. L. Rowell remembers Carroll's observing, happiness is always recognized in retrospect; see "By Miss H. L. Rowell," Appendix A, III, in Hudson, *Lewis Carroll*, pp. 318–322. The hour of conscious bliss of the dancing insects is definitely the exception.

where Arthur maintains that allowing children to amuse themselves with play on Sundays brings them closer to God than would forbidding play (I, 386).

The ideal of innocent playfulness is also reflected in the circumstance that the good characters are playful in manner and that other characters act playfully precisely when they are good. When the Narrator remarks at the outset of *Sylvie and Bruno Concluded* that the "sweet playfulness" of the fairy children spreads a magic radiance over his life (II, 1), this only sums up a leading feature of their charm, noted many times in passing. To mention one example, it is natural for the brother and sister to break through the barriers of dignified restraint surrounding the monarch of Dogland and to enjoy a "game of romps" with him (I, 181–182). Their motto in life is really "Pleasure first, and business afterwards" (II, 9); though Sylvie does spend much of her time persuading Bruno to get on with the business of lessons when all he wants to do is play, she is hardly very determined, and every reproof ends with a kiss and Bruno's having his way.

Sylvie is, as the introductory poem to *Sylvie and Bruno Concluded* has it, a "delicious Fay—/The guardian of a Sprite that lives to tease thee—/Loving in earnest, chiding but in play" (II, viii). Lady Muriel consistently displays the same "sweet playfulness" as the children (II, 293, also 24, 28, and others). Despite his predilection for expressing weighty sentiments, Arthur is likewise characterized by "playfulness" of manner (II, 280). Listening to them, the Narrator finds it "*exactly* like Sylvie talking to Bruno" (II, 118).

The point is once explicitly made that heaven may begin on earth for the simple and childlike. Thus in one of Sylvie's and Bruno's adventures with the Narrator in which they perform good to the neighborhood, the harried, nagging drunkard's wife turns suddenly "playful" after her burden is relieved by her husband's vow to quit drinking. Playfulness and youthfulness are equated (II, 89). Eric Lindon, Arthur's rival, rejected because of his shaky religion and marked out for an edifying semiconversion at the end, is unmistakably signaled as not all bad, for one thing, by the fact that he plays with Bruno (I, 267–268).

iv

However, Carroll's conception of play as basically games with rules of a highly competitive character inevitably gives a certain sharp edge even to the play of Sylvie and Bruno. (We should recall that Wonderland and Looking-Glass land are ruthless worlds. Although in noncompetitive situations Alice can demonstrate moral compunction, say, in not dropping the marmalade jar on whoever may be below or in caring for the Duchess's baby [*W*, pp. 27, 86], game contexts tend to dissipate her scruples; in the croquet game, for instance, she is notably without pity for either the Red Queen or the Duchess, both opponents.) This abrasive edge becomes apparent in Bruno's attitude, for of the brother and sister pair he is the less excessively good. Bruno is highly conscious of the rules governing all activities, and he is at times gingerly rebellious (as Alice gets to be) in the face of those he doesn't care for. He maintains that he cannot learn what he doesn't like but only when he freely chooses (II, 10).

Sylvie represents the voice of authority when she responds to Bruno's wish for fewer rules for lessons: " 'Yes, there *ought* to be such a lot of Rules, you wicked, wicked boy! And how dare you *think* at all about it?' " (II, 12). Bruno does dare to think and to challenge unpalatable codes. Nevertheless, he shows great deference to rules and authorities in those areas that he likes and accepts. One of his remarks to the Narrator reveals his game player's attitude, to which he is faithful even when it threatens his own well-being.[6] One day when the

---

[6] Bruno is no more in favor of cheating than Arthur, who quixotically defends gambling at whist in that it discourages demoralizing winking at

Narrator captures him by surprise in Kensington Gardens, Bruno states that he thinks it the Rule that someone who succeeds in catching a fairy has the right to eat him. But Bruno adds, as he isn't perfectly sure of this, the Narrator had better ask (II, 4–5).

The element of capital risk in such a game is obvious, and the relation of winning to eating up one's opponent. Bruno and Sylvie entertain themselves constantly throughout both books by arguing, clearly a competitive activity. That it is play undertaken for the fun of it is indicated by the analogy implied by Bruno's comment that he should have two heads, one for eating dinner, one for arguing with Sylvie (II, 10).) Arguing is his cure for tears, too (I, 308).

For loving sister and brother, the two are sharp, almost brutal with each other. Sylvie's tone in her fiat about rules, above, is not gentle. The "sweet" Sylvie is capable of telling a story ostensibly for Bruno's amusement, though in fact it frightens him sadly, all about a fat, juicy little boy named Bruno who is pursued by a lion (II, Chapter XIV). As a matter of fact, the stories told by both Sylvie and Bruno almost always concern one animal eating or trying to eat up another, with much emphasis on biting off or "nubbling" of heads.

Sylvie and Bruno are perpetually at each other in these novels. But it is very important to notice, as the Narrator reminds us, that theirs is a "new form of argument" that always ends in much hugging and kissing (II, 17). This is an abnormal ending for argument, which is after all a form of "collision." Its analogy to the physical collision of war is pointed out in Arthur's fanciful speculation on the possible communication between beings on a crescendo and diminuendo scale of relative size. To preserve fairness, argument would have to be substituted for war.

---

cheating, such as that notorious among young lady croquet players (II, 135).

In their playful collision Sylvie and Bruno stop short of that normal issue of competitive games, the triumph of one over the other. What intervenes is announced in the message that ends *Sylvie and Bruno Concluded:* "It is Love" (II, 411). The following is the refrain of Sylvie's and Bruno's song:

> For I think it is Love,
> For I feel it is Love,
> For I'm sure it is nothing but Love!   [II, 307]

Sylvie is the ultimate embodiment of altruism over egoism; like her counterpart Lady Muriel, she can be described as good, sweet, pure, true-hearted, and self-denying. An unpresuming child, she is very shy of being made much of at Lady Muriel's party by being asked to play the piano, but she does play for others' sakes: "I could see that she was resolved to forget herself, and do her best to give pleasure to Lady Muriel and her friends" (II, 76). Of course between the alternate sides of the magic locket Sylvie chooses "SYLVIE WILL LOVE ALL" over "ALL WILL LOVE SYLVIE" (II, 410). Nothing could be clearer; whether the message is entirely convincing is another matter.

What of the various playful beings with whom love cannot be relied upon to intercede? The conspiracy against Sylvie's and Bruno's father, so good he is made Elf King, is called a game—" 'What a game, oh, what a game,' " as the Chancellor remarks to his fellow players, the Vice-Warden and Vice-Wardeness (I, 49). The Vice-Warden delights in "playfully" shouting "Boh" at his wife, a goose if there ever was one (I, 119). Uggug, the son of the Vice-Warden and his lady, is likewise a playful creature. He exhibits his "dear child's playfulness" in emptying a dish of butter on Sylvie by way of a birthday surprise, for which he enjoys, at least briefly, exultation and "triumph" (I, 37–38). And he is suffered by his parents to confiscate Bruno's apple pudding and all his toys (I, 162).

The conspirators' game is stopped short by a miraculous next-to-last chapter conversion in which they see the wickedness of their ways and ask the Warden's forgiveness (II, 383). However, Uggug remains "loveless, loveless" (II, 386) and fulfills the destiny that might be expected from "His Exalted Fatness," "a hideous fat boy . . . with the expression of a prize pig" (I, 125, 23), by turning into a wild, prickly, porcupinish beast. This animal is "furious" (II, 389) (reminiscent of Fury and the Red Queens). He represents a kind of apotheosis of aggressiveness, something not wholly absent from Sylvie and Bruno, particularly Bruno, who, for instance, once plans to spoil Sylvie's garden because she makes him do lessons instead of letting him play (I, 200)), but Uggug's aggressiveness goes beyond the pale. The Narrator tells us that fairies have moral if childish natures (II, 301); Uggug appears to engulf his in rampaging bestiality.

The continuum linking playfulness, conceived in the form of games, and furious aggressiveness, constitutes a difficulty, I believe, for Carroll. He attempts to resolve it by providing for the intervention of love before the germ of aggressivity in play causes it to loose its innocence, an innocence he never denies. And yet he does certainly question the innocence of that form of play he calls sport. He is uneasy with the latter because it carries the implicit motive of self-aggrandizement into extreme destructiveness, of others and even of oneself. We may remember Sylvie's story of the three little foxes in a bag, one of whom ate up the other two and then ate up himself, so that there was nothing but a mouth left. But since the *Sylvie and Bruno* books are essentially sentimental, the story goes on to shake all the eaten out of the mouth of the eater and to terminate the three foxes in reformation (II, 239–246).

Both prefaces consider the issue of sport. Carroll's attitude is mixed, but for the most part negative. He says hunting down a man-eating tiger may yield legitimate exultation, but not seeking one's pleasure in the easy slaughter of defenseless creatures (I, xx). When he treats the "Morality of Sport" in his second preface, Carroll confesses there is too much pro and con to cover, but he states his conclusion, that the infliction of pain, when there is no necessity, is cruel and wrong (II, xviii).

Infliction of pain is a form of mastery, which when striven for without necessity makes an activity into play. That Carroll rejects the extreme manifestation of the destructive aspect of play can be gathered from the *Sylvie and Bruno* books and from other pieces that touch on sport like "Some Popular Fallacies About Vivisection," although unfortunately he never completed an essay exclusively on sport which he projected in the preface to *Sylvie and Bruno Concluded*.

V

Discussion, of sport, particularly of hunting, is scattered through the *Sylvie and Bruno* books. An extended scene shows Sylvie's lamentation—" 'And GOD meant your life to be so beautiful!' "—over a hare that has been "Hunted to death" (I, 320). " 'I thought hunting was a thing they *played* at— like a game,' " she says. She has experience of one type of hunting, for snails, but she and Bruno never kill them (I, 318). In fact, in an earlier scene, the Narrator had been unable to detect anything wrong with such a hunt, even though there was no "use" in it (I, 211). Nevertheless, he makes a distinction between the fairies' game and sport: " 'How am I to get the idea of *Sport* into your innocent mind?' " he reflects (I, 318). His explanation goes over the same ground covered in the preface: the evil transference from the hunting of fierce animals who are a match for man to the hunting of timid, guiltless ones, whom he ought to love, not kill (I, 319).

There are a number of comic variations on the sport theme. One is the account by the eccentric old man, Mein Herr, of the sport of Cub-Hunting, in which universities compete against each other in running down (literally) the best scholars. The sport offers a satiric epitome of the hectic snowballing of competition, which finally makes prey of human beings (II, 187–193). Mein Herr also satirizes competition in the variety of forms exported to his country by the "British" system. He demonstrates the disastrous counterproductiveness in agriculture, commerce, military affairs, and especially politics of the "Dichotomy-Principle," a mental set of "chronic hostility" that makes all these activities into versions of war (II, 196–208).

Another parable of sport occurs in the Professor's song about "The little man that had a little gun," a story of a duck hunt in a hunting world,

> Where the Grublet is sought by the Froglet:
> Where Frog is pursued by the Duck:
> Where the Ducklet is chased by the Doglet—
> So runs the world's luck!

Although the duck is eventually shot and carried home for dinner, two stanzas briefly threaten a turning of the animals upon the hunter: "'Avengement,' they cry, 'on our Foelet!'" (II, 265–269). This threat is taken up again in comic form in *The Hunting of the Snark*.

In several stanzas of another poem, "The Pig-Tale," we can descry through the disjunction of the nonsense a continuity having to do again with the theme of victim/victimizer:

> Little Birds are bathing
> Crocodiles in cream,
> Like a happy dream:
> Like, but not so lasting—
> Crocodiles, when fasting,
> Are not all they seem!
>
> . . . . .
> Little Birds are choking
> Baronets with bun,
> Taught to fire a gun:

Taught, I say, to splinter
Salmon in the winter—
Merely for the fun.   [II, 371, 377]

I want to be light-handed in interpreting bits of a fantasia isolated from their context (if a fantasia can be said to provide a context), but I do find intimations to this effect: here is a crocodile-eat-bird world; to think otherwise is a "happy dream"; but one way to avoid being the fun for someone else is to seek it oneself in the shape of choking instead of feeding, of firing guns and hunting fishes.

So much for roundabout comic commentary. For the most part the treatment of sport in the *Sylvie and Bruno* books is straightforward and dead serious. One of Arthur's long speeches concerns the difficulty of justifying the suffering of innocents. One might understand a man overdriving a horse, for that is clearly a case of self-interested, practical sin. But what about a cat playing with a mouse, where there is presumably no purpose at all (II, 296–297)? Arthur here raises the question of an inborn impulse of creatures to dominate others even when utilitarian self-interest is lacking. Arthur consistently denies that utilitarianism explains motivation. For example, he scorns recommendations to virtue by Dr. Watts and Paley which claim that morality is the best policy; Arthur contends that's not true, and that moral feeling must be based on something more than a profit and loss concept of religion, if any but the stupid are to be moral (I, 235–236, 274–276). The corollary is also implied that cruelty need be as little founded on utilitarian motives as virtue. This is a frightening doctrine: evil as well as good impulses come spontaneously. The impulse to disinterested cruelty finds expression in hunting, but that it is an element in game playing in general is suggested by the fact that the cat and mouse are said to play at a game.

Bruno recounts the cat's version of the encounter between himself and the mouse: " 'I teaches the Mouses new games:

the Mouses likes it ever so much. . . . Sometimes little accidents happens: sometimes the Mouses kill theirselves!' " (II, 361). The cat rationalizes the activity as a game by the fiction that it is reciprocal, that the mouse wishes to play. We may suspect that the mouse does not, that the activity is not an even-steven game entered into freely by both parties, but rather a hunt, where all odds and all desire to play are on one side. Carroll has shown us before in the *Alices* the tendency of games to become thus unbalanced. And he makes very clear in the *Sylvie and Bruno* novels his disapproval of such sport.

In an intriguing passage Lady Muriel laments for Arthur (supposed dead doing "God's work" in a plague-ridden village, II, 278) in the very same words as Sylvie's lament for the hunted hare: " 'And God meant your life to be so beautiful!' " (II, 291). Lady Muriel's words in conjunction with those they echo seem almost to suggest (if this linking is thematic and not just formally whimsical—which is always hard to determine in these novels) that Arthur, like the hare, has been in some sense hunted to death. Is God himself a cruel hunter, and are we his defenseless victims? (Arthur is certainly as innocent as the hare.) The suggestion makes understandable one of the Narrator's comments, grim for a happy-ending fairy story: "Human life seems, on the whole, to contain more of sorrow than of joy. And yet the world goes on. Who knows why?" (II, 119). It helps explain why the work contains the insight that "live" is just "evil" spelled backward (II, 11–12). Such an attitude is exactly opposite that which conceives of life as an hour's dance of conscious bliss. It issues, at least in part, from the darker side of Carroll's conception of play, the side that poses the question whether play, so fundamentally human, may not exfoliate a certain innate malevolence, and whether, in fact, we ourselves may not be the playthings of some malevolent higher consciousness.[7]

[7] Such a god sounds like Caliban's in Browning's "Caliban upon Setebos."

These questions are unresolved in the *Alices*. The Red
King's role remains as a somewhat sinister riddle at the end of
Looking-Glass, although on the positive side it is suggested
that Alice can learn to master rather than be mastered by
games. But the resolutions in *Sylvie and Bruno* and *Sylvie and
Bruno Concluded* are the less satisfying for being forced in
favor of the positive. Magical hurricane-force powers foil the
wicked game of conspiracy in Outland. And it turns out that
Arthur has not died after all but has been saved—by whom?
by his very rival—to be happily restored to love and Lady
Muriel. She and the reader can simply forget about any implied indictment of God for a hunter's cruelty.

In spite of the aggressiveness, even cruelty, that Carroll
shows to be imbedded in the purely disinterested and very
human activity of play (he once told a little girl that *Alice* was
about "malice"),[8] in its game and sport versions, he still finishes his last novels with a not very convincing conclusion,
supportive of a sentimental belief, or desire to believe, in what
Arthur calls Original Goodness (I, 276). In spite of everything
he has shown to undermine it, he never completely abandons
an ideal of the innocence of play.

Carroll and Sport and *The Hunting of the Snark*

Though he was an inventor of countless games, we have
Carroll's word that he was "no sportsman" (*Works*, p. 1193).[9]
The field sport that he most insistently decries is hunting, in
its several forms. But he also wrote a poem (in the manner of

---

[8] Carroll, *Letters*, to Dolly Argyles, Nov. 28, 1867, pp. 48–49. Florence
Becker Lennon has remarked the uncontrolled tension between sadism and
sentimentality in the *Sylvie and Bruno* books (*Victoria through the Looking-
Glass*, p. 216).

[9] Carroll, "Some Popular Fallacies about Vivisection," *Works*, pp. 1189–
1201; references in the text.

Goldsmith) opposing conversion of portions of the University Parks into cricket grounds. "The Deserted Parks" (1867) argues against the encroachment of "one selfish pastime," "exclusive sports," upon the grounds rightly to be enjoyed by all. It attacks the unhealthy "luxury," compared to wine, of heady pleasure-seeking sport, which would gobble up space and trample the park into an "arid waste" for its own gratification. Carroll's stand is clear; he raises his voice "even aginst the potent spell of "Play!"[10]

But hunting remains the type of play that epitomizes all that Carroll feared and denounced in sport. His tract "Some Popular Fallacies about Vivisection" (1875) offers an intriguing argument built on, the commonly raised analogy between vivisection and hunting. Carroll says he would not be anxious to refute this analogy if all who condemned vivisection were also to condemn hunting. But, suspecting that the analogy is oftenest used to justify both, he proposes to examine it critically (*Works,* p. 1192).

He adamantly refuses to defend sports: "Especially for hunting, I have no defense to offer"; he believes that it involves great cruelty (*Works,* p. 1193). But at least a good huntsman shoots an animal and spares it protracted pain, and this cannot be said of the vivisectionist, Carroll alleges. He reports reasons for believing that audiences actually enjoy vivisectionist lectures, including the spectacle of the writhing animals, which may be compared to the spectacle offered in the cruel sport of bullfighting (*Works,* p. 1195).

Carroll does not object to the suffering of the animals so much as to the brutalization of the men who learn to observe it with equanimity or even with pleasure (*Works,* p. 1194). His charge is serious: "Much of the excitement and interest of sport depends on causes entirely unconnected with the infliction of pain, which is rather ignored than deliberately con-

[10] Carroll (Anonymous), rprt. in *The Humorous Verse of Lewis Carroll,* pp. 250–253.

templated; whereas in vivisection the painful effects constitute in many cases a part, in some cases the whole, of the interest felt by the spectator" (*Works*, p. 1196). He explicitly identifies the human trait that he fears: "It is a humiliating but an undeniable truth, that man has something of the wild beast in him, that a thirst for blood can be aroused in him by witnessing a scene of carnage"; a deadening of revulsion via familiarity may develop into indifference, morbid interest, "then a positive pleasure, and then a ghastly and ferocious delight" (*Works*, p. 1195).

A point of special interest in this tract is Carroll's conviction that vivisection, a science, and generally regarded as work, may actually proceed on the same sort of motivation as that to be found in sport. He refutes the vivisector's argument that whereas the motive of the sportsman is "mere pleasure," his own is the advancement of science and the good of humanity: "It is my conviction that the non-scientific world is far too ready to attribute to the advocates of science all the virtues they are so ready to claim" (*Works*, p. 1196). He gives evidence from his own experience that much so-called work is undertaken for its own sake and thus detached from the moral realm just as much as if it were a form of play: "As one who has himself devoted much time and labour to scientific investigations, I desire to offer the strongest possible protest against this falsely coloured picture [science as motivated by altruistic duty]. I believe that any branch of science, when taken up by one who has a natural turn for it, will soon become as fascinating as sport to the ardent sportsman, or as any form of pleasure to the most refined sensualist. The claim that hard work, or the endurance of privation, proves the existence of an unselfish motive, is simply monstrous" (*Works*, p. 1197).

Carroll suspects that a "craving for more knowledge, *whether useful or useless* [italics mine], which is as natural an appetite as the craving for novelty or any other form of excitement" is just as likely to be the scientist's motive as the desire to serve mankind (*Works*, p. 1197). Carroll can conceive of all manner of activities, even those usually revered as the most hard-working and altruistic, as essentially selfish. They may be undertaken for their own sakes, for the pleasure of mental mastery (notice the language of incorporation employed in the quotation above), and be quite possibly as useless to all purposes other than psychological gratification as the most gratuitous play.

Carroll concludes by denying that the toleration of one form of evil—for example, sport—necessitates the toleration of others—for example, vivisection (*Works*, p. 1197). He sees no reason why scientists who feed their craving for knowledge at the expense of animals should not someday do so at the expense of human beings, particularly as long as their investigations are protected under the false labels of duty and work (*Works*, pp. 1200–1201). This treatise exposes fallacies not only in popular opinions about vivisection but also in the popular Victorian "gospel of work"; that is, much that is respected because it involves dedication, hard labor, and so on, is no more deserving of respect than certain species of play. As has been observed, Carroll treats sport as the ultimate manifestation of an amoral and self-aggrandizing strain in play and games. He almost always conceives of the more harmless forms of play as aggressively goal-oriented and competitive: the goal is the triumph of one by means of the defeat of the other. This may be acceptable, up to a point innocent (as long as the rules hold and both sides are willing), but the same cannot be said for triumph via infliction of pain and death, as in the sport of hunting.

The *Alices* show how the energy of cat and mouse running through play works to erode the restraints of a game system until the game becomes a pseudogame. After that the game is a hunt, returning to something like the original condition of unmediated assimilation. Alice may have a relatively civilized mentality, which though sufficiently disillusioned by experi-

ence to learn not to fall patsy to others' stacked games, is yet
not become cynical enough to learn to stack her own. Carroll
does not demonstrate how she can maintain this fine balance of
civilization, although he apparently believes that fair games
can still be played, for whereas in *Wonderland* Alice merely
demolishes a false game, in *Looking-Glass* she attests to the
continued power of a true one; she wins by asserting the rules
of chess. Even if she is a little girl capable of covertly threaten-
ing mice and birds with Dinah the cat, it is hard to imagine
Alice becoming a Red Queen. Only later does Carroll name
the force capable of preserving the innocence of play from its
psychologically built-in impulse to destructiveness. In *Sylvia
and Bruno* and *Sylvie and Bruno Concluded* love intervenes
and saves the day. On the other hand, in "Some Popular
Fallacies about Vivisection" Carroll warns us not to count on
any magical intervention when we find ourselves under the
knife of a vivisector, who is as disinterestedly intent on what
he is doing as any sportsman (*Works*, p. 1201). Nothing intervenes either in *The Hunting of the Snark.*

Although *The Hunting of the Snark* (1876) has for the most
part been interpreted as a quest[11] rather than as a hunt, the

---

[11] See, for example, W. H. Auden, *The Enchaféd Flood or The Ro-
mantic Iconography of the Sea* (New York, 1950), p. 17; he cites the
Snark to exemplify the quest out onto the limitlessness of the sea. Gilbert
Murray, in his foreword to *The Hunting of the Snark by Lewis Carroll,
Translated into Latin Elegaics with Translator's Note Appended on the
Inner Meaning of the Poem and Other Things* by H. D. Watson (Oxford,
1936), interprets it as a search for peace (p. vii). Watson's note mentions
in addition the search-for-happiness reading, accepted after the fact by
Carroll (see his letter cited in Collingwood, *Life and Letters*, p. 173), as
well as the search-for-the-absolute interpretation (pp. 58–61). Percival
Robert Brinton's preface to *The Hunting of the Snark by Lewis Carroll
Rendered into Latin Verse* (London, 1934) compares the Bellman's quest
to Aeneas' (p. v). Lennon interprets the *Snark* as an oedipal quest (pp.
176f). For a summary of other interpretations, see Michael Holquist,
"What Is a Boojum? Language and Modernism," *Yale French Studies*,
XLIII (Winter 1969), 145–169.

hunt theme is worth considering, for the poem suggests again Carroll's sense of the destructive part of play, which may turn back on the player.

A passage in Carroll's "Journal of a Tour in Russia in 1867," like the Professor's song of the hunted duck and the "Avengement" of the animals in *Sylvie and Bruno Concluded,* throws some light on the *Snark.* At the Hermitage in St. Petersburg, Carroll saw a painting by Paul Potter representing, he records, "with extraordinary skill & humor, in compartments, hunting-scenes of various kinds of game, the lion, boar, &c.—and the final combination of all the animals to try & execute the hunter and his dogs."[12] The painting visualizes the same turning of the tables of the hunted upon the hunter as is described in the *Snark,* where the hunted *Snark,* turning out to be a Boojum, causes the utter destruction, in fact, the vanishing away, of the Baker, one of the hunters.

A game, besides growing more and more destructive of those outside oneself, may become self-destructive. In another interesting passage in the "Russian Journal" Carroll describes an intense type of play, not literally a hunt but presented with an image from the hunt. Again the players become by a strange transformation the victims: "We visited the evening concert, & found play (rouge-et-noir &c) going on in an adjoining room, & it was a very interesting sight for novices to watch. There was but little feeling to detect in the faces of the gamblers, even when they lost heavily: what was to be seen was only momentary, & all the more intense for being suppressed. . . . some old, some quite young, & all absorbed & with a fascinated look like helpless creatures magnetised by the gaze of a beast of prey."[13]

The moral judgment conveyed by the *Snark* is of course

---

[12] Carroll, July 31, "Journal of a Tour in Russia in 1867," in McDermott, ed., *The Russian Journal,* p. 90.

[13] Carroll, Sept. 5, 1867, *ibid,* p. 118.

much less obvious than that in this passage or in the *Sylvie and Bruno* novels. Carroll is tongue in cheek about announcing the "strong moral purpose" of his "instructive poem" in the preface (*HS*, p. 5).[14] The arithmetical principles and natural history he promises to inculcate consist mainly of the Rule of Three—"what I tell you three times is true" (*HS*, p. 9)—and a lesson on the attributes of the Jubjub bird in "Fit the Fifth." And of course later in " 'Alice' on the Stage" Carroll disclaims any inkling of the meaning of the *Snark*.[15]

All we know is that it is a hunt upon the high seas, apparently motivated solely by the Bellman's whimsical determination. Even when danger is forecast by the Baker—what if the Snark is a Boojum?—the Bellman refuses to allow any "debate" on whether or not to continue the hunt. Discussion would be absurd," for the "Snark is at hand"; he urges an unspecified "duty," what "England expects," upon his crew (*HS*, pp. 27–29). They agree. In the heat of their enthusiasm the Butcher forgets his love for killing Beavers, and he and the Beaver become the closest of hunting companions. The Barrister's aggressiveness against the Beaver is likewise diverted by his dream of the Snark (*HS*, pp. 38–40).

This interesting dream depicts the prey, the Snark, in a position similar to that of the animals who put on trial and then execute their hunters in Paul Potter's painting. In the dream the hunters are not themselves being tried; the defendant is a pig. What is significant is that the Snark takes on the functions of lawyer, jury, and judge (like Fury in the Mouse's Tale, like the Queen of Hearts and the Red Queen in the *Alices*). And the tables are completely turned: beginning as a

---

[14] *The Hunting of the Snark: An Agony in Eight Fits*, illus. Henry Holiday (New York, 1899); hereafter identified in the text as *HS*, with page reference.

[15] Carroll, " 'Alice' on the Stage," *The Theatre* (April 1887), rprt. in Collingwood, ed., *Diversions and Digressions*, pp. 167–168.

lawyer for the defense of the pig, he ends by pronouncing his own client guilty (*HS*, pp. 40–44).

The "Banker's Fate" forecasts the Baker's. In his "zeal to discover the Snark," the Banker rushes ahead and is caught by a Bandersnatch. This is so terrifying that the Banker goes quite mad (*HS*, pp. 46–49). He is mentally destroyed; he may be said to have lost his head. Rather than a conqueror, he is a victim in the hunt.

The epic ends with the complete physical destruction of one of the hunters, as prefigured in his dream fight with the Snark (*HS*, pp. 23–25). The Baker, "in the midst of his laughter and glee," just when he has found the Snark to the "delight" of the others—their worst fear is "that the chase might fail"—suddenly becomes its victim. "For the Snark *was* a Boojum, you see" (*HS*, pp. 50–53).

7. A Victorian Gospel of Amusement?

The following is too typical of commentaries on Carroll's books: " 'Alice' possesses the first title to greatness required of a Victorian work—namely, that it is not Victorian."[1] Jerome Buckley rightly points out in *The Victorian Temper* that the time has passed for the debunking of the age and the salvaging of particular authors as anomalies.[2] Certainly Carroll was a Victorian. However, our ordinary view of Victorianism may be so restricted that it does not bring Carroll into range. We hear a great deal about the gospel of work, but what about play during the reign of Victoria?

The Victorians enjoyed themselves, in spite of the gospel of work and the absence of a section on play, games, sport, leisure, recreation, pastime, or amusement in Walter Houghton's *The Victorian Frame of Mind*. The lack is partly explained by the fact that Houghton begins at 1830—by which time Carlyle had espoused his celebrated work ethic—and ends with 1870, when Carroll had only just published and the

[1] Guy Boas, "Alice," *Blackwood's*, CCXLII (Dec. 1937), 740.

[2] Buckley, "Victorianism," in *The Victorian Temper* (Cambridge, Mass., 1951), pp. 1–13, rprt. in *Backgrounds in Victorian Literature*, ed. Richard A. Levine (San Francisco, 1967), p. 44. Kathleen Tillotson has pointed out the responsibility of Carroll's critics to place him in the context of Victorianism in "Lewis Carroll and the Kitten on the Hearth," *English*, VIII (Autumn 1950), 136–138.

late Victorians were yet to come. It would be a mistake to identify the frame of mind he describes with the entire Victorian period; much remains to be said beyond the statement, "except for 'God,' the most popular word in the Victorian vocabulary must have been 'work.' " An article in *The Spectator* of 1889 tells us that "The Gospel of Amusement" "seems of late years to have come to the front with a sort of a rush." And in the middle of Houghton's time span, in 1861, we can find attestations to the rise of this doctrine. Says A. Wynter in the magazine *Once a Week*, considering the well-known earnestness of the Victorian image, "I have lived in the belief that we were fallen on evil days, when 'All work and no play makes Jack a dull boy.' Our working population have the reputation, throughout Europe, of being a dull heavy people, in whose highlows the elastic spirit of sport no longer treads." But on picking up one of the numerous sporting-life journals, *Bell's Life*, which had been thriving for a third of a century (and which, incidentally, had received an article by Lewis Carroll on betting, considered from a purely mathematical standpoint, in 1857), he learned otherwise: "Why, what has become of the dull boy, Jack? Is this the individual, I asked myself, whom I find running, racing, diving, swimming, shooting, rattling, dog-fighting, knurring and spelling, cricketing, quoiting, racketing, &c., &c.?" Wynter concludes that it is only the great middle class that have not been given to sports, thereby generating the impression that the old sports and pastimes had died out. Other commentators reversed this analysis and thought the lower classes worse off than the middle, precisely because the latter were accustomed to squelch amusements within the former even more than it did within itself. But Wynter was not alone in thinking society at large to be moving in the direction which he saw laid out in the pages of *Bell's Life*, and not alone in thinking this movement constituted a great "amendment in our public life."[3]

[3] Houghton, *The Victorian Frame of Mind* (New Haven, London, 1957),

Of course the position the middle class was moving from, whether taken to define its own habits or those it enforced on its laborers, was the gospel of work, which we may file under Carlyle's name.

Interestingly enough, Carlyle himself for a time espoused a doctrine of play, one running along aesthetic lines from the German Romantics, though it dwindled till it was hardly to be noticed in later works such as *Past and Present* (1843) and the *Reminiscences* (1881). Carlyle discusses Schiller's *Aesthetic Letters* in his *Life of Schiller* (1825), and although he stresses Schiller's morality, he also strongly endorses the antiutilitarianism of his aesthetic theory. The influence of Schiller's idea of art as play may be well observed in Carlyle's two essays on Jean-Paul Richter (1827, 1830), whose intricately whimsical style strongly influenced his own. He specifically invokes the *Aesthetic Letters* to describe Richter. For instance, he says the highest expression of genius is to be found in its sport. He admires Richter's exuberance, his wild levity, his playfulness, the "sportful harmony" of his prose.[4]

But even here Carlyle insists on Richter's morality, which suggests the line he is taking away from a pure ideal of gratuitous play in art. His treatment of Goethe also reveals this direction. He admonishes the reader to "Close thy *Byron;* open thy *Goethe*" in *Sartor Resartus* (1833), reflecting his view in the essay on Goethe of 1828, where he praises Goethe for turning away from self-indulgence and toward earnestness and duty.[5]

p. 242; "The Gospel of Amusement," *Spectator*, LXIII (1889), 547; Wynter, " 'Bell's Life' and Our Sports and Pastimes," *Once a Week*, V (1861), 151–153; on Carroll's betting article see Collingwood, *Life and Letters*, p. 69.

4 Carlyle, *The Works of Thomas Carlyle*, ed. with notes H. D. Traill, Centenary ed. (London, 1899–1901), XXV, 112–114, and "Jean Paul Friedrich Richter Again," *Works*, XXVII, 121; see too his "Jean Paul Friedrich Richter," *Works*, XXVI, 1–25.

5 Carlyle, *Sartor Resartus: The Life and Opinions of Herr Teufelsdröckh*,

Eventually Carlyle arrived at a position which throws doubt on his whole artistic enterprise. In *Past and Present* he distinguishes sharply between work and play: "Life was never a May-game for men: in all times the lot of the dumb millions born to toil was defaced with manifold sufferings, injustices, heavy burdens, avoidable and unavoidable; not play at all, but hard work." For all the bizarre playfulness of his style, Carlyle came to abominate playful, self-indulgent, nonuseful schools of literature (for that matter throwing question on the usefulness and therefore the validity of literature in general). He had a low opinion of Charles Lamb, frequently noted for a whimsical style, a predilection for nonearnest, sometimes termed trivial, topics, a devaluation of work, an antimoralistic approach to children's literature, whom, in fact, Walter Pater recognized as an early practitioner of art for art's sake. Carlyle found in Lamb an unhealthy lack of moral earnestness; he was too skittishly humorous and playful. For by the time of the *Reminiscences,* where Carlyle discusses Lamb, he had turned his back on an ideal either of life or art as play.[6]

Whatever gospel of play was to be inherited from the German Romantics or found as a native legacy, for example in Lamb, was in the end soundly disowned by one of the most listened-to seers instituting the Victorian age. Carlyle, along with the conjunction of the Evangelical and Utilitarian movements and the arrival of Prince Albert from the prim court of Saxe-Coburg-Gotha, we are often enough told, produced the earnest Victorians.

---

ed. Charles Frederich Harrold (New York, 1937), p. 192, and his "Goethe," *Works,* XXVI, 198–257. See also Carlyle's "Goethe's Helena" (1828), *Works,* XXVI, 146–197, for a discussion of *Faust,* unfinished at that time; Carlyle projects Faust's salvation by art as but a step, salvation by practical moral action to follow after.

[6] Carlyle, *Past and Present,* ed. Richard Altick (Boston, 1965), pp. 209–210, and *Reminiscences,* ed. Charles Eliot Norton, 2 vols in 1 (London, 1887), I, 94; Pater, "Charles Lamb," in *Appreciations with an Essay on Style* (London, 1910), p. 110.

Carroll did not oppose the gospel of work head on; he only cast it into some question. He has at Wordsworth's "Resolution and Independence," which urges a sort of protogospel of work, though he never takes on Carlyle directly. Collingwood tells us that Carroll's rule of life was that biblical injunction beloved by Carlyle, "Whatsoever thy hand findeth to do, do it with all thy might." He quotes a letter of Carroll's containing the rest of the text, "The night cometh, when no man can work." Although critics and biographers do not mention Carroll's reading much of Carlyle, he apparently accepted some of the famous leading ideas. For example, he wrote in a letter, "I have read very little of 'Sartor Resartus,' and don't know the passage you quote: but I accept the idea of the material body being the 'dress' of the spiritual—a dress needed for material life."[7]

However, Carlyle's ideas on work and Carroll's differ significantly. *Past and Present* celebrates the fact that it is the duty of the slave Gurth to do the work that Cedric commands of him. Carlyle stresses the obligation for the generality of men to do what work is at hand, as imposed by God's delegates on earth, his heroes.[8] Carroll, on the other hand, in *Sylvie and Bruno Concluded* defends the rights of what he terms "idle mouths." No human law exercises the right to demand work of the idle; only a divine law has that power (II, 37–40). This law, he implies, can only assert itself internally, from within the individual man. It cannot be enforced by one man upon another. Carroll thus rejects any gospel of enforced work, which Carlyle is quite willing to urge upon the non-heroes of the world.

Carroll may well have been himself an overconscientious worker, as Florence Becker Lennon calls him. T. B. Strong says he fell frequently into paroxysms of work. Indeed, his biog-

---

[7] Collingwood, *Life and Letters*, pp. 292, 242.
[8] Carlyle, *Past and Present*, pp. 211–212.

raphers all call attention to his industrious habits, and their view is to a large extent confirmed in the diaries, although these characteristically dwell on work projected but not done or not done well, and work yet to do. Especially in the early diaries Carroll makes lists of reading and other labors to be performed, which, as a matter of fact, he seldom succeeded in finishing. He formed many New Year's resolutions, making, for example, "a list of things to be learned by heart and kept up at such times as Railway-travelling, etc.," and asking himself, "What do I propose as the work of the New Year? . . . Constant improvements of habits of activity, punctuality." An entry from his diary illustrates how the measure of the gospel of work caused him to suffer under an endemic sense of short-coming: "Here, at the close of another year, how much of neglect, carelessness, and sin have I to remember! I had hoped, during the year, to have made a beginning in parochial work, to have thrown off habits of evil, to have advanced in my work at Christ Church. How little, next to nothing, has been done of all this!" In the years that followed Carroll continued to have difficulty living up to his resolutions. He writes, for instance, in a diary entry in 1882, "Work is hard to keep up by the sea, when it is all voluntary. I must try for better habits."[9]

Hudson tells us that Carroll took little interest in games at Rugby. As we know, he held in low esteem the kind of brutal good-sportsmanship so closely related to fighting which is cele-brated for instance in Thomas Hughes's famous *Tom Brown's Schooldays* (1857). Carroll was so serious-minded that he not only refused dinner invitations in later years to conserve time and energy for the projects he wanted to finish before he died, but once even went so far as to record in his diary an aversion

[9] Lennon, *Victoria through the Looking-Glass*, p. 85; Strong, "Lewis Carroll," *Cornhill Magazine*, IV n.s. (March 1898), 303–310, rprt. in *Aspects of Alice*, ed. Phillips, p. 40; Carroll, *Diaries*, Dec. 31, 1857, Dec. 31, 1863, and Aug. 17, 1882, I, 136, 208; II, 409.

185

to playing parlor games with adults because he considered them a waste of time. (Children seemed better justifiers of frivolity, or maybe they retained more of the authentic play spirit. At any rate, Carroll thought music a form of play more suitable for adult parties.)[10]

In spite of his seriousness, Carroll definitely did not approve of work done merely out of duty externally imposed and against the grain. He says he learned much at Rugby but little *"con amore."* We may recall two lines in his parody of Tennyson, "The Palace of Humbug" (1855), in which he paints a gloomy picture of the teacher

> Who wasteth childhood's happy day
> In work more profitless than play.

He suspected that much that is respected as work is no more deserving of its high repute than if it were play. Of his labors as a mathematical lecturer at Christ Church he says, "It is thankless, uphill work, goading unwilling men to learning they have no taste for." He had no faith in the value of driving men along the path of duty. Like Charles Lamb, who under rather similar circumstances found it possible to retire early from his toil at East India House, Carroll experienced a great release when he quit his enforced labors in order to do what was his own work, writing. He thought a man does his best when he works for love's sake, rather than from ulterior motives. Carroll opposed alienated labor.[11]

Labor was not alienated for the child actors who were his special friends. He felt they acted out of a strong inborn pas-

[10] Hudson, *Lewis Carroll*, pp. 48, 210–211; Carroll, *Diaries*, May 30, 1882, II, 406.

[11] See Carroll, *Diaries*, 1832–1854, I, 13–14; Carroll, "Lays of Mystery, Imagination, and Humour, No. I," from *Mischmasch* (1855–1862), *The Rectory Umbrella and Mischmasch*, pp. 136–138, rprt. in *The Humorous Verse of Lewis Carroll*, pp. 39–41; Carroll, *Diaries*, Nov. 26, 1856, I, 96; Hudson, p. 258.

sion of their natures (spontaneously, as in play); hence their work was done "*con amore,*" and they rejoiced in it intensely. In his diary Carroll observes that these children seem not to be working at all, but rather enjoying themselves. They worked according to what might be called a gospel of play, which Carroll admired.[12]

An early statement of Carroll's in a letter home to his family suggests something of the playfulness of his attitude about his own accomplishments. He says that when he took honors at Oxford, he felt like a child with a new toy. As Belle Moses' biography recognizes, "Lewis Carroll was a hard worker, but fame came to him without an effort. . . . It was when he played that he reached the heights." Carroll approaches the philosophy expressed by that late-century apologist for idlers, Robert Louis Stevenson: "As if a man's soul were not small enough to begin with, they [the drudgers of the world] have dwarfed and narrowed theirs by a life of all work and no play." "They do not take pleasure in the exercise of their faculties for its own sake. . . . When they do not require to go to office, when they are not hungry and have no mind to drink, the whole breathing world is a blank to them." "There is no duty we so much underrate as the duty of being happy." Not every Victorian was always an earnest Victorian.[13]

[12] Carroll, letter to *The St. James Gazette* (July 16, 1887), quoted in Collingwood, *Life and Letters,* pp. 180–181; see also Carroll's letter of Aug. 4, 1889, in which he defends the right of stage children to act professionally, as it is an innocent, healthy occupation which they love, in *Diaries,* II, 473; Carroll, *Diaries,* March 1, 1867, I, 252.

[13] Carroll, letter quoted in Collingwood, *Life and Letters,* p. 58; Moses, *Lewis Carroll in Wonderland and at Home: The Story of His Life* (London, New York, 1910), p. 144; Stevenson, "An Apology for Idlers," *The Works of Robert Lewis Stevenson,* South Seas ed. (New York, 1925), II, 64–66. A testament to Stevenson's sustained power of play exists in a compilation called "Stevenson at Play: War Correspondence from Stevenson's Notebook," pref. Lloyd Osbourne, rprt. from *Scribner's,* XXVI (1898), in *Works,* XXVII, 357–377. This documents a tin-soldier and dice

John Ruskin is known as one of the less frivolous. Yet he has something to say in favor of play in a lecture published in *The Crown of Wild Olive* (1866), something that is usually lost sight of, especially since the title of the lecture in question is "Work." Ruskin is not at all against play; in fact he is for it. What he is against is anyone's being able to play because others work. He pronounces a social principle—that all should earn so that all can play: "The possible quantity of play depends on the possible quantity of pay." Ruskin points to the irony of a certain colloquial understanding of the word "play," that is, being laid up with sickness. "This is what you have brought the word 'play' to mean, in the heart of merry England!" And he says that the people of England, all too appropriately known as the working class, should get play in this life as well as in the next. Much of the message in this and the next lecture in the series, "Traffic," concerns the uselessness and pointlessness of the work that deprives men of their leisure and almost of their humanity. Like Carroll, unlike Carlyle, Ruskin stands for unalienated labor: "The entire object of true education is to make people not merely *do* the right things [what Cedric will settle for if only Gurth can be made to go in the way that is right] but *enjoy* the right things—not merely industrious, but to love industry." The desideratum of the working frame of mind is to retain the cheerfulness of the child. The child is Ruskin's ideal, as he was for many in the

---

war game that Stevenson carried on for weeks on end with the twelve-year-old Lloyd Osbourne. He expended remarkable ingenuity in recreating the real conditions of war in an attic at Davos, although his advantage was weakened by Osbourne's superiority with the pop-gun, the fire power of the war. All the movements of the troops, all the exploits of the generals, Piffle, Potty, Pipes, and Napoleon were recorded in Stevenson's notebook in the form of verisimilar articles and editorials from two fictitious newspapers. A *jeu d'esprit* in the literal sense. Stevenson also memorialized the paper toy theaters popular in the period in "A Penny Plain and Two Pence Coloured," *Works*, XIII, 114–121.

latter part of the nineteenth century—"always ready for play —beautiful play,—for lovely human play is like the play of the Sun."[14]

Let us look at the play of some of these Victorian children, who were idealized—the cult of the child is obvious in the *Sylvie and Bruno* books—partly because they never forgot how to do it. And we will discover among adult Victorians too a good deal of the play that Mr. Ruskin wanted and that Mr. Wynter of *Once a Week* expected to see a lot more of.

Probably the best place to look at the playthings of the nineteenth century (and the most elaborate ones may not have been just for the children) is in the beautiful Swiss picture book *The Golden Age of Toys* by Jac Remise and Jean Fondin,[15] illustrating the products of the toymakers' industry, which was growing with the rest of industry—phenomenally. The book is European in scope; different countries had different specialties and broad export trade. Musical boxes and automata came out of Switzerland; cheap clockwork and pasteboard toys (some of the first toy soldiers, only later to be tin) originated in Germany; magic lanterns, most famous of the many illusionist toys (with lovely names like thaumotrope, phenakistiscope, zoëtrope, praxinoscope, panoptic panorama, kaleidoscope), came from France; and England was a great maker of "penny toys" of tin, wood, composition, feather, and wire, of toy theaters and all other sorts of paper cutouts imaginable, remembered as "penny plain, two pence coloured."

---

[14] "Work," *The Works of John Ruskin*, ed. E. T. Cook and Alexander Wedderburn (London, 1905), XVIII, 409, 422, 418, 430–431, and "Traffic," *Works*, XVIII, 435–436.

[15] Remise and Fondin, *The Golden Age of Toys*, trans. D. B. Tubbs (Lausanne, Switzerland, 1967). For a contemporary account of the London toy-making industry, see Henry Mayhew, *Voices of the Poor: Selections from the Morning Chronicle 'Labour and the Poor' (1849–1850)*, Cass Library of Victorian Times no. 10, ed. Anne Humphreys (London, 1971), pp. 157–178.

The industrial revolution made toys available from the plushest nursery to the street corner. It also heavily influenced the kinds of toys available; the market kept itself modern. For example, in the late 1840's model railways followed in the tracks of real ones, and in the course of the century they followed as well the advance of technology, from clockwork, to steam, to electricity. Toy boats suited the times, accurately representing changing styles as mercantile fleets shifted from sail to steam in the sixties, and as navy fashions developed, war after war. The industrial revolution actually entered the playroom, especially with steam-driven toys, as whole factories were there reconstructed. Victorian toys aimed at brilliant verisimilitude, up-to-date technology, and scientific/historical educationalism. Dolls were naturalistic; they learned to blink with wired eyes early in the century and to issue lifelike cries from imbedded music-box devices; they had scale-model houses built for them, precise to the teathings (by 1900 there were toy bathrooms) ; and they were dressed in the miniature perfection of the latest mode by a big-time doll industry, one of whose outwork operatives is to be remembered in the Doll's Dressmaker of *Our Mutual Friend*. A child had to be quite an able engineer to handle lubrication, filling, spirit lamp, temperature and pressure, and clean-up on his small but real steam engine and to avoid nasty accidents. He could learn a good deal by watching the gyrations of his toy acrobat, motivated by the motion of a light metal fan set going by a candle's heat. Praxinoscope shows might combine magical effects (as also the many magic acts retailed to the young) with instruction, in the subjects represented by the moving images, and in the principle to be grasped behind the motion. Bright, lacquered automata or even simple paper cutouts might recreate current notabilities like the Tichbourne Claimant or scenes from the Boer War.

Remise and Fondin observe that this was the golden age, toys abounded, and "parents showed a preference for objects which could be related to current events or recent inventions."

And yet, at least according to an article in *The Contemporary Review* (which also, by the way, reviews *Alice*), children preferred old toys, because new ones, with their fullness of color and definiteness of form, left little scope for the exercise of the fancy. But fancy is not easily kept down, and if there were not better, there were more toys to stimulate it. It is likely that a compromise was effected and that children took the play out of the instructive playthings offered and let the instruction ride.[16]

The notable book on the period's board games is F. R. B. Whitehouse's *Table Games of Georgian and Victorian Days*. These games were not originally on boards at all but rolled up like maps; in fact, mapmakers made them. It is little wonder that there a great many geographical games, various Tours, as Through America, Of England and Wales, Round the World. The earliest dated game known is A Journey through Europe (1759), and it is simply an engraving of the map of Europe, with four rules for moves printed alongside and with instructions that "the Journey through Europe is to be played in all respects the same as the game of the Goose."[17]

The Game of the Goose was the prototype of the racetrack type of board game, usually featuring an anticlockwise snail-shell track; it is generally supposed to have been introduced from France in the mid-eighteenth century. (The other main type of board game, less common, was the pay and receive game.) Goose itself, in which one moves as the dice dictate from one space to the next, encountering simple setbacks and advances as one lands upon one or the other of the thirteen goose-inscribed spaces, is a game of pure amusement. The geese teach no lesson. It is easy to see though how the racetrack model can be made to yield instructional byproducts,

[16] Remise and Fondin, p. 111; "Children and Children's Books," *Contemporary Review*, XI (1869), 12. Beryl Platts' "Improving the Victorian Child," *Country Life*, CXL (1966), 1472, 1475, also suggests that children escaped too much improvement and contrived to enjoy themselves.

[17] Whitehouse, *Table Games of Georgian and Victorian Days* (London, 1951), p. 7.

as in geographical versions, also in historical. Playing the Royal Geneological Pastime of the Sovereigns of England, one proceeds toward victory over fifty-two shields giving the names, dates, and faces of the monarchs. This Georgian game exemplifies the instructive type. According to its accompanying text, "Most games are calculated only to promote little Arts and Cunning [like cards or unmodified Goose perhaps] but this while it will undoubtedly amuse will not a little contribute to make the Players acquainted with the geneology of their own kings." Facts were inculcated and interpretations too, as in the later Royal Game of British Sovereigns, whose winning square reads "Victoria. May her reign be long and happy," or as in the triangle-shaped racetrack game called The Pyramid of History, where queen and family form the apex.[18]

In addition to such instructional games as Useful Knowledge, Learning in Sport, The Pence Table, The Great Exhibition, Produce and Manufacture of England & Wales, The Naturalist, Grammatical Game in Rhyme, there were games of moral improvement. One of the most moral is The Game of Human Life of 1790, which insists that the teetotum must be marked with numbers one through six upon purchase, above all things "to avoid introducing a Dice Box into private Families." But ten years later a game such as The Mansion of Happiness could, without shame, direct the use of a pair of dice. The nineteenth century was, if anything, loosening up in its suspicion of games and all things to do with them. Late in the century there was less of the animus that one finds in this legend to one of the pictures of the 1804 game Science in Sport or The Pleasures of Astronomy: "The County Goal—this is the place for those who attend to the motions of Billiard Balls more than to the motions of the planets." Why, the heroines of Charlotte Yonge's irreproachable novels play billiards.[19]

Several Victorian table games represented the child's path

18 Whitehouse, pp. 25, 26.
19 Whitehouse, pp. 47, 35.

among virtues and vices, and while proclaiming that "Virtue is its Own Reward" at the winning end, reinforced this written precept with an unwritten one, namely, virtue means winning and vice versa. There is a good deal of what Victorians called emulation embodied in the form and approved in the texts of their games. We find the race (The Hare and the Tortoise), the power struggle (Russia versus Turkey), the worthiness of competition (Emulation), the aspiration/attainment/progress syndrome (The Hill of Science—An Allegory). Games enforced the benefits of winning (Race to the Gold Diggings of Australia, Virtue Rewarded and Vice Punished).

In spite of everything, Victorian games were less concerned with overt messages than Georgian games had been. Whitehouse says that William Spooner, one of the great early Victorian game publishers, devoted at least half his output to pure amusement.[20] So the Game of the Goose was reissued, along with noninstructional games of the Snake, of Cupid, of the Monkey. Backgammon, a Carroll favorite, is the best-known descendant of Goose. We encounter names like The Adventures of Lord Pudding, Waddling Frog, and Fortunio and His Seven Gifted Servants.

While many Victorian table games were "improving," they were probably less bound to improve than their forbears. Increasingly available, games I suspect tended to disseminate the following two lessons as much as any others: that competition is fun and can pay off, and that all sorts of things, from history to arithmetic to The Game of Human Life, can be fun as games are fun, another way of saying that anything can be played. In his *Self-Help* (1859) Samuel Smiles doubtless correctly estimated, while decrying, one effect upon young Victorian players: "Learning their knowledge and science in sport, they will be too apt to make sport of both."[21]

[20] Whitehouse, p. 53.
[21] Smiles, *Self-Help, With Illustrations of Conduct and Perseverance*, introd. Asa Briggs, Centenary ed. (London, 1958), p. 311.

The further resources of the child in pursuit of entertainment were many. There were spillikins, marbles, spelling bees, charades, and word games. The term "jigsaw puzzle" was invented in the ninteenth century. There were hobbies: pressing flowers, mineralogical cabinets, stamp albums, scrapbooks. There were pets. Private theatricals and musical evenings were popular, as any reader of nineteenth-century novels knows.[22]

One of the purposes of a recent book by Stella Margetson called *Leisure and Pleasure in the Nineteenth Century* is to testify that both existed, as the prerogative of the upper classes and the off-day right of the masses. If country fairs were on the decline, Derby Days were on the rise; if the old pleasure gardens like Vauxhall and Cremorne were deteriorating to be finally suppressed, places like Hampstead Heath provided their lack. Following the Great Exhibition a multitude of resorts of family amusement were assured of success. Tussaud's Waxworks is ony the most famous (maybe sharing the honor with Mrs. Jarley's in *The Old Curiosity Shop*). Other such were Alexandra Palace, the Royal Aquarium, Westminster, the Brighton Aquarium, Astley's Circus, and Egyptian Hall, where one might witness Bullock's Natural History Collections, Belzoni's Egyptian Discoveries, or one of the very popular illusionist displays of Albert Smith, perhaps The Ascent of Mont Blanc.[23]

The number of museums and concerts was on the increase. Articles in leading journals pleaded for faster increase in wholesome amusements. Music halls, though plentiful, were not felt

[22] See F. Gordon Roe, *The Victorian Child*, illus. Iris Brooke (London, 1959), pp. 31–44.

[23] Margetson, *Leisure and Pleasure in the Nineteenth Century* (New York, 1969); Roe, pp. 120–136. Recall that the sport of mountain climbing is largely of 19th-century British origin; see Edward Whymper's *Scrambles amongst the Alps in the Years 1860–69* and Leslie Stephens' *The Playground of Europe*, both from 1871. See also for Victorian recreations Geoffey Best, "Society at Play," *Mid-Victorian Britain 1851–1875* (New York, 1972), pp. 197–227.

to offer proper family entertainment. More proper were the offerings of the theaters, Covent Gardens, Drury Lane, Haymarket, St. James, Savoy, Lyceum, and others, which in addition to Shakespeare and the serious repertoire presented opéra bouffe, burlesque, musical comedy, pantomime, farce, and ballet. Many dramatic productions were suitable and actually tailored for children, as we can tell by the fact that Lewis Carroll took so many children to see them.[24]

A combination of things launched the institution of the seaside holiday resort. Bathing came first into prominence because of King George III's ill health, and it developed from remedy to recreation in the course of the century. The Prince Regent was addicted to Brighton and its pleasures; many other Englishmen came to be so also (Carroll favored Sandown and Eastbourne), for increased leisure time and cheap excursion trains made this possible. For children, the pleasures included, besides dousings from bathing machines, spades and buckets, goat-chaise and donkey rides, "nigger mistrels," hurdy-gurdies, Punch and Judy, peepshows, magic-lantern and camera-obscura shows. All enjoyed one major Victorian contribution to the festivity of the seaside resort, the pier, part promenade, part carnival.[25]

But one did not need to travel by rail from home to enjoy oneself. Among the most important of Victorian recreations were outdoor games. These supplemented hoops, kites, skating, riding, walking (think how much time people in novels spend walking), later bicycling. Bowls, quoits, battledore and shuttlecock, badminton, table and lawn tennis, golf, archery and croquet. Take just the last two in this partial list. Archery was a real fad, especially among young ladies and curates, says an article on "Our Amusements" from *Blackwood's* in 1866

[24] Roe, pp. 120–136.

[25] *Ibid.*, and Keith Spence, "The Pleasures of the Pier," *Country Life*, CXLI (1967), 1086, 1089, 1091.

'(remember the elegant archery meeting in *Daniel Deronda*). And if we didn't know it well enough from Carroll, "a great revolution has been made in the summer life of country society by the introduction of croquet. . . . It is a sign of a want which must have been pretty generally felt, that such a very mild invention should have been hailed as a social revolution. . . . Go where one will, whole families and their visitors are seen mallet in hand, whose great object in life, from the little girl of six to the grandpapa of sixty, seems to be to get through their hoops." The century set itself to supplying for as many as possible the felt want of recreation. Cricket was of course the "sport paramount," and in 1855 *The Boys' Own Book* says that everybody was playing it: "No less strange than true—young matrons have played Matches of Criquet against maidens, having husbands, brothers, and sweethearts for their spectators."[26]

There was a deepening respect and a heightening enthusiasm for team sports in the second half of the nineteenth century, and if some were enjoyed at home during the holidays, the source of the cult resided in the public schools. Each school had its specialty in cricket and football.[27] The school tablet of one William Webb Ellis records the honor that he it was who first took the ball in his arms and ran, so originating the distinctive feature of the Rugby game, this supposedly in 1823.[28] The Rugby match is the center of the school experience in Hughes's *Tom Brown's Schooldays*, and, this much-read and taken-to-heart work would have us believe, the center and radiating point of its hero's whole life as a true Victorian gen-

---

[26] "Our Amusements," *Blackwood's*, C (1866), 710, 707–708; from *The Boy's Own Book: A Complete Encyclopedia of All the Diversions, Athletic, Scientific, and Recreative, of Boyhood and Youth* (London, 1855), in Nigel Temple, sel. and introd., *Seen and Not Heard: A Garland of Fancies for Victorian Children* (New York, 1970), pp. 162–163.

[27] Roe, pp. 110–113.

[28] Vernon Bartlett, *The Past of Pastimes* (Edinburgh, 1969), p. 94.

tleman. Games were "an opportunity specially devised by Providence to enable small boys to work off their original sin," according to one headmaster. In *Young Victorians* Marion Lochhead tells us that there existed in the schools a "preference for a *mystique* of games rather than any mystical devotion." They provided a large chunk of the ethics of the period; it is safe to extend the well-known saying of the Duke of Wellington and assert that many fought and died by the team principle learned at Rugby, Harrow, and Eton, whether it be at Waterloo, in the Crimean or Boer Wars, or in World War I.[29]

Girls gradually benefited from the cult of games, as their education went the course from the elegant to the serious to the athletic (a saying of Janet Hogarth in the nineties). Whereas in the 1850's Elizabeth Wordsworth deplored the lack of exercise which girls might have had in games instead of pouring their spirits into silliness, dress, and flirting, by the nineties a faith in games as productive of England's greatness prevailed among female educators like Miss Dove, who wrote "Cultivation of the Body," and Mrs. Beale, who edited *Work and Play in Girls' Schools.*[30]

A quaint illustration of the importance of games to Victorians appears in an intimate record of child life by Eleanor Farjeon, *A Nursery in the Nineties.* The children of the Farjeon household lived by a multitude of self-concocted game rules governing all aspects of life. A game called So-and-So was designed (and elaborately) to formalize, regulate, and eventually terminate disputes. Good-Night, God-Bless-You, Dear Papa and Mama amounted to a contest between the child endeavoring to say good-night and family antagonists still below stairs as to whether she could complete the agreed-upon verbal formula before the top step. The Sneezing and Hiccup Championship is pretty well self-explanatory. Such spontane-

[29] Lochhead, *Young Victorians* (London, 1959), pp. 72, 157–158, 233–234.

[30] Lochhead, pp. 199, 103–104, 229.

ous and pervasive game playing is not surprising to find in a family which so modeled itself upon the sporting sectarianism of the times and of the nation that each child was born into the world as either Oxford or Cambridge and assumed a hereditary obligation to root for its school during that most famous of boatraces. Herbert Maxwell says in *Blackwood's* in 1892 (the article is entitled "Games"), "Nor if love of amusement may be considered one of the characteristics of youth, is there any sign of approaching senility; for the ingenuity in providing pastimes, and the ardour with which they are followed, have never in any age been exceeded."[31]

We incline to forget, what with the publicity given the Victorian gospel of work, that "They Taught the World to Play," according to the title of an essay by Sir Charles Tennyson in *Victorian Studies*. There is no need for me to prolong comment on the Marylebone Criquet Club, in existence since 1787, the Football Association of 1863, the English Rugby Union of 1871, the All-England Croquet Club at Wimbleton of 1869, in 1877 to be the All-England Croquet and Lawn Tennis Club. They testify to the same spirit as do, say, the first international England/Scotland draughts match in 1884 and the reestablishment of the Olympic games in 1896, in which the English Amateur Athletic Association played an important role. Tennyson claims, in fact, that in stimulating interest, disseminating knowledge, organizing, and regularizing rules and penalties, particularly in all manner of ball games (but boxing, competitive rowing, and yachting were very British too), nineteenth-century England "was the world's games-master."[32]

We can see reflected in the journals a steady rise in concern for amusements, athletics, games, sport. William Poole's Index

[31] Farjeon, *A Nursery in the Nineties* (London, 1960), pp. 297–312; Maxwell, "Games," *Blackwood's*, CLII (1892), 406.

[32] Bartlett, pp. 39–100; Tennyson, "They Taught the World to Play," *Victorian Studies*, II (March 1959), 211–222.

of nineteenth-century periodical literature lists as many articles on the last-named subject appearing between the years 1892–1896, as it does for the seventy-five-year-longer period 1802–1881. Several main trends emerge from these articles. One is simply a recognition of the increase in leisure and pastime brought about by amelioration of social conditions and a shift in social attitudes. Walter Besant says in *The Contemporary Review* in 1884 that workmen no longer confine their expectations of life to a hovel and enough to eat. And too, their masters have changed in the last forty years: "We must remember how very little play went on even among the comfortable and opulent classes in those days." Since then has occurred a "gradual recognition of the great natural law that men and women, as well as boys and girls, must have play."[33]

Besant was a leader among those who applauded the extension of amusements and said they should extend even further —to the East End of London, for instance. So also Godfrey Turner in *The Nineteenth Century* (1877), who asserts that the old puritanical repression of play was a mistake; more (and wholesome) public amusements are needed. We find articles with titles like "Methods of Social Reform, Amusements of the People." ("The old idea of keeping people moral by keeping their noses at the grindstone must be abandoned.") We find pleas of the sort by the Earl of Meath in *The Nineteenth Century* calling for "Public Playgrounds for Children."[34]

Amusements, exercise, games, and sport were defended for improving health and morals. Lord Brabazon prescribes the

---

[33] Besant, "The Amusements of the People," *Contemporary Review*, VL (1884), 342, 347.

[34] Says "The Gospel of Amusement," p. 547, Walter Besant "makes of the doctrine of amusement a new gospel." Turner, "Amusements of the English People," *Nineteenth Century*, II (1877), 820–830; W. Stanley Jevons, "Methods of Social Reform, Amusements of the People," *Contemporary Review*, XXXIII (1878), 502; Earl of Meath, "Public Playgrounds for Children," *Nineteenth Century*, XXXIV (1893), 267–271.

new concept of "physical education" as the antidote to "Decay of Bodily Strength in Towns." He argues that healthier bodies mean healthier minds, hence better success at manufacture, on which England's position in the world depends. Hely Hutchinson Almond considers "Football as a Moral Agent." Lawn tennis, cycling, and gymnastics may do more for women's rights than any other factor, he observes. Why but because health and strength bring mental and social progress. Considering, he says, the degenerating state of our breathlessly overpacked cities, civilization seems almost doomed but that health, virtue, and temperance are being taught to their inhabitants: "From this point of view it is well for this crowded little island of ours that the athletic movement has assumed such a universal and irresistible form as it has done in the case of football." Almond contends that football educates in the spirit of chivalry, fairness, and good temper. The spectator too may be uplifted by watching it, he feels sure, although professionalism is an attendant evil of the movement that must be combated, so that hopefully the Rugby game can be saved from the demoralization of the Association game.[35]

Most of the above arguments for play and games are utilitarian in one form or another. True, there was an increased admission that when it comes right down to it work is hateful and undertaken only out of necessity; and there is something in human nature that craves play—just as much among the working classes as among the others. And yet, for example, one article that makes this argument, Maxwell's "Games" (1892), goes on to stress the function of games for yielding rest and instruction useful in the rest of life.[36] (Recall that this is the period of Karl Groos and the German education-by-play

[35] Brabazon, "Decay of Bodily Strength in Towns," *Nineteenth Century*, XXI (1887), 673–676; Almond, "Football as a Moral Agent," *Nineteenth Century*, XXXIV (1893), 899–911.

[36] Maxwell, pp. 406, 418.

movement, with their combination of appreciation of play and emphasis on functionalism.)

The utility argument for sports in the nineteenth century has been analyzed in Bruce Haley's interesting essay "Sports and the Victorian World." He traces the worship of athletics from Dr. Arnold and Rugby to the various sporting clubs and leagues, and he pinpoints the philosophy behind the faith as that of "Mens Sana in Corpore Sano." This was a commonplace of the time, probably most famously espoused in Hughes's *Tom Brown's Schooldays,* and in the "muscular Christianity" of Charles Kingsley, say in *Two Years Ago* (1857). These narratives demonstrate that the manly sporting type turns out to be the true gentleman and Christian after all. Even Samuel Smiles, who as a rule disapproved of pleasure, commended sports for their cultivation of mind and body. The philosophy takes doctrinal form in Herbert Spencer's *Education: Intellectual, Moral, Physical* (1861). He announces that "the first requisite to success in life is 'to be a good animal,' and to be a nation of good animals is the first condition of national prosperity." Spencer recognizes his affinities with Kingsley. These are manifest, for as in *Two Years Ago* the benighted evangelist who preaches do-nothing fatalism in the face of the cholera is deemed worthy of death (he is appropriately struck blue with the disease himself) for this sin against the well-being of the town, so Spencer presents preservation of health as a "duty": obeying nature's dictates in the upkeep of the animal mechanism is "physical morality," its opposite "physical sin." Already in 1860 Spencer felt assured that "To the importance of bodily exercise most people are to some degree awake." His purpose was to bring them more fully to their senses in the areas of girls' education and the physical culture of little children at home. Assuming that a sound body must precede a sound mind, and adhering to that familiar nineteenth-century model, the conservation of energy, Spencer deduces that excess concentration on the mental robs the body of its due, and "it is fatal to that vigor of *physique* which is needful to make intellectual training available in the struggle of life."[37]

The struggle of life, a key idea. Darwin derived his alternate term for natural selection from Spencer, the "survival of the fittest." He speaks in addition in terms of the struggle for life, the struggle for existence, the race for life, the law of battle, battle within battle, the war of nature. Darwin's world view is one of competition above all. Self-interest and destruction go with it. The consolations Darwin offers are that fear is not felt, death is prompt, and "the vigorous, the healthy, and the happy survive and multiply." Spencer's and Kingsley's positions fitted well with comfort like this; that is, they assumed that the strong, healthy human animal (the athletic type) turns out most "fit" in an intellectual/moral sense too. But Thomas Huxley was worried over the introduction of the phrase "survival of the fittest" into the *Origin*'s fifth edition because fittest suggests best or highest, whereas he thought natural selection might just as well operate toward degradation, at least ethically speaking. (It may not be stretching things to suspect that Carroll was having his joke at a version of the wrong-way possibility of evolution in *Sylvie and Bruno*. There Lady Muriel and the Narrator agree that a principle appears to be at work in modern literature, particularly of the railway-train genre, that evolves so to speak an elephant into a mouse [I, 64–65].)[38]

[37] Spencer, *Education: Intellectual, Moral, Physical* (New York, 1896), pp. 222, 223, 282–283, 252, 276; Kingsley, *Two Years Ago* (London, 1906), 293–294. And see Haley, "Sports and the Victorian World," *Western Humanities Review*, XXII (1968), 115–125; Smiles, *Self-Help*, p. 303; Hughes, *Tom Brown's Schooldays* (London, 1906).

[38] Charles Darwin, *The Origin of Species*, ed. Morse Peckham, Variorum ed. (Philadelphia, 1959), pp. 145, 162; James Allen Rogers, "Darwinism and Social Darwinism," *Journal of the History of Ideas*, XXXIII (1972), 278, citing *The Life and Letters of Thomas Huxley*, ed. Leonard Huxley, 2 vols. (New York, 1901), II, 284.

Many Victorians came to learn the painfulness of the implications of *The Origin of Species*. Darwin himself says, "Nothing is easier to admit in words than the truth of the universal struggle for life, or more difficult—at least I have found it so—than constantly to bear this conclusion in mind." Especially as applied to man. Huxey came in time to a conviction just opposite social darwinism—with which Spencer is associated—that the history of society, of civilization, is the record of men's attempts to establish limits on the struggle for existence.[39]

One of the outstanding refuters or would-be forgers of compromise with Darwin was the eminent Catholic scientist, St. George Mivart, whose *On the Genesis of the Species* (1871) Carroll and many others appreciated for reconciling evolution and God. (Mivart broke with his friend and teacher Huxley over this rending issue of the times.) Mivart accomplishes his reconciliation by reducing natural selection to the status of merely one of several forces in the development of species and by reinstating through the piling up of careful biological evidence the respectability of the older teleological world view, with its implicit belief in divine purpose, hence in the advance of all life toward the good, moral as well as physical. In particular Mivart draws the line at mere physical explanation when it comes to man. Man's soul is direct from God; it is not to be accounted for according to the processes that account for material phenomena, including man's body. Mivart devotes a section to "Evolution and Ethics," in which he shows that man's moral sense cannot be explained by utilitarian (survival) factors. Like Arthur in Carroll's *Sylvie and Bruno Concluded*, Mivart holds it nonsense to think men are moral because crime does not pay. Crime does, more often than not, but man has been given an innate moral sense which

<hr>

[39] Darwin, p. 146; Thomas Huxley, "The Struggle for Existence, A Programme," *Nineteenth Century*, XXIII (1888), 161–180.

acts quite outside the precincts of self-interest. It can be characterized as basically altruistic. The red-in-tooth-and-claw aspect of nature doesn't disturb Mivart much because that simply poses the old problem of evil. The problem he wants to answer and combat is the age's "ready acceptance of the great doctrine concerning the essential bestiality of man."[40]

Mivart claims that the existence of an aesthetic faculty as well as of a moral one counters gross darwinism because both show a strata of human experience above the struggle for existence.[41] We may extrapolate from Mivart on the subject of play, which is allied to the aesthetic, if Schiller is right. Play is not part of the struggle for existence. Does that raise it into a realm of sweetness and light? Maybe, even though a functionalist can say that there are material benefits to be derived from play even if not aimed at; it makes one fit. But there is a further possibility: what if play, dissociated from all conscious motivation of utility, recapitulates for the very fun of it the struggle for existence? What if Spencer is right in "Aesthetic Sentiments": "Love of conquest, so dominant in all creatures because it is the correlative of success in the struggle for existence, gets gratification from a victory at chess in the absence of ruder victories"? What if self-seeking, competitiveness, and aggression blossom for their own sakes in play? Carroll didn't want these things to be so in their worst sense, but he intended to write an essay questioning the morality of sport which would have joined many other articles in the journals during the latter part of the century which were raising the same question.

Haley's "Sports and the Victorian World" shows us where to look for the reaction against sports beginning in the mid-

[40] Mivart, *On the Genesis of the Species* (New York, 1871), p. 221; Mivart, *Contemporary Evolution: An Essay on Some Recent Social Changes* (New York, 1876), p. 165; see also Jacob W. Gruber, *A Conscience in Conflict: The Life of St. George Mivart* (New York, 1960).

[41] Mivart, *Genesis*, pp. 296–297.

1860's. For instance, the Public School Commission announced doubts whether the athletic movement wasn't getting out of hand. *Punch* caricatures of sportsmen made their appearance. As an antitype to Tom Thurnall of *Two Years Ago*, Wilkie Collins reveals the sportsman Geoffrey Delamayn—"a magnificent human animal, wrought up to the highest pitch of human development, from head to foot" by the modern educational system, and a national hero as stroke-oar in a University boatrace—to be a callous brute and intended murderer in *Man and Wife* (1870). Says a spokesman for the older, wiser generation in the novel, whose primary hate is sport, though he also takes a dim view of croquet and other such new-fangled substitutes for rational social intercourse: " 'I don't like the model young Briton. . . . There is far too much glorification in England, just now, of the mere physical qualities which an Englishman shares with the savage and the brute. . . . Read the popular books—attend the popular amusements; and you will find at the bottom of them all a lessening regard for the gentler graces of civilized life, and a growing admiration for the virtues of the aboriginal Briton!' " In a like vein if more mildly, Matthew Arnold urges the limitations of being a Barbarian and caring nothing but for field sports, manly exercises, the body's vigor, and good looks.[42]

And then the journals. The subject of amusement/athletics took its place as one worthy of the most serious. Asks *The Spectator* (1889), "Is not the theory that amusement is an indispensable part of life getting pushed nowadays a little too far?" A writer in *The Contemporary Review* (1866) approves

---

[42] Haley, 119–120; Collins, *Man and Wife, The Works of Wilkie Collins* (New York, n.d.), III, 67, 78–81; Arnold, *Culture and Anarchy: An Essay on Political and Social Criticism*, ed. Ian Gregor (Indianapolis, New York, 1971), p. 85. Add here the pleasant irony of Matthew Arnold's interest in fishing and in his own appearance. Everyone had to draw the line somewhere. Often it was between fishing and hunting, between healthful exercise and muscle-building fanaticism. Arnold was no Barbarian.

in part of what athletics is supposed to do, deplores what it actually does: many parents and schoolmasters "recommend a boy to make himself temperate and strong, not that he may run a manly and Christian course through the world, but that he may run better than A or B at the next Oxford and Cambridge sports." Another writer, in *The Nineteenth Century*, puts the savageness of the competition in a stronger light. In "The New Football Mania" (1892) he says, "The new football is a far more effectual arouser of the unregenerate passions of mankind than either a political gathering or a race meeting." He reminds us that if one side wins, the other loses, and drunken fighting ensues. An American journal, *Every Saturday*, applauds the reaction against athletics spearheaded by *Man and Wife*: "The Morality of Muscularity" (1870) doubts whether the "fierce competition" of modern sports does not "inflict positive moral injury, by developing an animal intensity of the will—the root of one kind of cruelty." In fact, this article finds that Collins overstresses the physical evils attending muscular training in itself, but understresses the moral evils attending sporting competition: self-will, envy, vanity, greed.[43]

It was a full-blown controversy, and field sports were the center of it. E. A. Freeman wrote a crusading article in *The Fortnightly Review* on the morality of field sports, showing that they boasted very little. He expresses dismay at the doctrine that if man makes animals his prey, this only extends the normal law of hunting and killing which governs the animal world. He rejects the philosophical justification that "an impulse to destruction" forms part of the "order of nature." A version of such a justification is invoked by Anthony Trollope, who answers Freeman in the same volume of *The Fortnightly*

[43] "The Gospel of Amusement," 547; "Athletics," *Contemporary Review*, III (1866), 389; "The New Football Mania," *Nineteenth Century*, XXXII (1892), 622; The Morality of Muscularity," *Every Saturday: An Illustrated Journal of Choice Reading*, I, n.s. (1870), 525–526.

Review: suffering is part of nature, and "death is ever being turned into a matter of amusement." Other items in Trollope's defense of hunting are its beneficial effects for man, overriding what the animals may feel, and the fact that the fox probably owes his very existence to the sport that calls for his death. Freeman was answered again in *Temple Bar*, where it is maintained that "The Cruelty of Sportsmen" is a fallacy, or at least that the amount of pleasure derived by the hunters exceeds the amount of pain suffered by the hunted. An article in *Tinsley's Magazine* takes a light approach. Noting the animated contest over the compatibility of field sports with refinement or kindliness of heart, it cannot help wondering at the sportsman's claim that animals enjoy being hunted: "We wish the intelligent hare who assisted at the tea-party in Wonderland had given his sentiments on the subject." Whatever these might be, the writer feels certain that the poor men who fall victim to the game law as enforced by rabid sportsmen do not enjoy it.[44]

The Westminster Review carried impassioned articles like Florence Dixie's "The Horrors of Sport" (1892), which documents the agonies of pursued animals the world over and the author's agonies upon looking into their dying eyes after shooting them. The incitement to sport "is a remnant of barbarism in our natures," and the only hope is that "the day must dawn when that savage instinct will become eradicated." Likewise H. S. Salt in "Cruel Sports," *Westminster Review* (1893): "Whereas on other lines there has been a considerable amount of humane progress during the last thirty or forty years, which has taken visible effect in legislation—as, for example, in the rules and restrictions concerning cattle traffic, knackers' yards,

---

[44] Freeman, "The Morality of Field Sports," *Fortnightly Review*, VI, n.s. (1869), 353–385, and in the same volume, Trollope, "Mr. Freeman and the Morality of Hunting," 616–625; "The Cruelty of Sportsmen," *Temple Bar*, XXVIII (1870), 359–370; "The Characteristics of Sportsmen," *Tinsley's Magazine*, VI (1870), 291, 295.

vivisection, and the general treatment of all animals recognized as 'domestic'—there has been no corresponding improvement in the modes and methods of sport. Since the Acts of 1849 and 1854, there has been no further mitigation of our national love of 'killing something.' "[45]

The faith was not dead—the faith in progress of humanitarianism—that had animated a major book on play of 1831, Horatio Smith's *Festivals Games and Amustments, Ancient and Modern*. Its thesis is that man's recreations are an index of his ascent from barbarism and brutality. But in the second half of the century one had Darwin to contend with. One had the poet laureate's witness to "the blind wild-beast of force, / Whose home is in the sinews of a man." One had Ruskin asserting that war is the ultimate game, where "the natural restlessness and love of contest among men are disciplined, by consent, into modes of beautiful—though it may be fatal— play"; but that the pleasure (because the consent) easily goes bad, for as war is the extension of boys' pop-guns, "the worst of it is, that what was play to you when boys, was not play to the sparrows." How then preserve the faith in the regeneracy of the impulse to play, burgeoning into new forms and popular prominence all around?[46]

We have been considering mainly the possible viciousness of sports. A remarkable story by Christina Rossetti reminds us that this viciousness can characterize the games of children too. (Christina Rossetti was a friend, photographed and much

[45] Dixie, "The Horrors of Sport," *Westminster Review*, CXXXVII (1892), 49–52; Salt, "Cruel Sports," *Westminster Review*, CXXXX (1893), 545.

[46] Smith, with additions by Samuel Woodworth, *Festivals Games and Amusements, Ancient and Modern* (New York, 1862). Alfred Lord Tennyson, *The Princess*, introd. Albert S. Cook (Boston, 1902), p. 127, V, ll. 256–257 (Tennyson became poet laureate three years after the 1847 publication of *The Princess*); Ruskin, "War," *The Crown of Wild Olive, Works*, XVIII, 465, and "Traffic," *Works*, XVIII, 439.

admired by Carroll.) *Speaking Likenesses* (1874) bears some striking likenesses to *Alice*, except for the moralizing frame— the tale is told to keep a group of little girls at their needles. Flora is the birthday girl and is having a party where the guests are "to play pleasantly together. Well, we shall see." The blindman's buff turns to a wrangle; the tea party falls into bickering; Flora is finally so weary of her spoiled birthday that she falls asleep and dreams herself into a magic room where the evils of bad temper in play unfold to their very worst by way of a lesson. One boy at the dream party is prickled all over like a porcupine, another faceted at sharp angles, another is covered with hooks; one girl exudes slime, another is sticky from head to foot. They are gathered for a birthday feast, but Flora is not allowed to have a sip or a swallow. She is an accommodating child and declares herself willing to play at any game they like if only they will teach her how. The response is to call for a game named Hunt the Pincushion, which consists of chasing the smallest, weakest member of the group (preferably one with a hump, adds the narrator) so as to stick pins in her. Flora is It. If she suffers, so do her tormentors, for prickles, angles, hooks, slime, and stickiness can do a great deal of damage in a general melee. The next game is wonderfully titled Self-Help. Here the boys are the players, the girls the played. The object is to capture a victim by one's own best means (prickles, hooks, etc.). Says the narrator, bringing home the point to her audience, "I have seen before how very rough cruel play, if it can be termed play." The only one who enjoys herself is the dream's birthday queen, who stands aloof while the rest lay each other low. The final game is a stone-hurling battle in the play yard that becomes so violent that Flora at last wakes up. Altogether it is grim little tale, and games are seen in a grim light. This is not the "pleasant land of Play" of Robert Louis Stevenson's *A Child's Garden of Verses* (1885). That book stresses the positive aspect of play: its gift of power to the child, power enabling him to create a whole world, "My Kingdom," of the small household or garden environment where he is, in actuality, weak and subject to the adult "who never seems to want to play." The negative and positive are related, however, for Stevenson's lonely children play at a species of Self-Help, though it can be a far different thing when others are involved, play turns to games, and games break the bounds of decent restraints.[47]

There are two dangers in play. One is that it is purely self-motivated and self-gratifying, unrelated to extrinsic claims, which cuts it off from the stabilizing laws of work and duty. The other is that it is selfish, as eating is, a matter of pleasure in exerting one's own power, and can often, naturally enough, turn destructive.

The Victorians had a way of life, especially clear in the upper and middle classes and more especially among groups most excluded from work, young people and women, that depended upon an elaborate round of daily amusement. Read a novel by Charlotte Yonge (another friend of Carroll's, in whose impeccable *Monthly Packet* his stories appeared, including the prototype of *Sylvie and Bruno*). In *The Heir of Redclyffe* (1853) we find that unless something happens like family illness (which does happen often, and when it doesn't, fancy work and mental improvement help keep time occupied), there is nothing much for the characters to do or for the novelist to describe besides walking, riding, sketching, balls, singing, reading, pets, concerts, dancing lessons, parties, tea-drinkings out of doors, play-haymakings, battledore and shuttlecock, games of word definitions, billiards, and whatever diversion parlor and garden have to offer. Yes, the intensely moral heroines of Charotte Yonge play billiards, even though the great cloud over the head of the heir of Redclyffe which

---

[47] Rossetti, *Speaking Likenesses* (London, 1874), pp. 5, 33; Stevenson, "The Little Land" and "The Gardener," *A Child's Garden of Verses, Works,* XIV, 37, 47.

sets up and enables the entire plot derives from a suspicion that he games. Why are billiards all right, in this context? Because the good daughter Amy plays them with her father to please *him*. Play thereby loses its onus of selfishness and begins to look like work and duty. By the same token, the saint-like hero Guy, after staying away from a ball on the sudden conviction that it amounts to an indulgence and a distraction from mathematics and Greek, comes later to realize that he erred because he must consider his *friends'* pleasure in seeing *his* pleasure.[48] When Guy departs this world, his widow Amy learns that even her grief is a temptation to wrong, for what is right is to join in the usual family amusements, thinking of others instead of herself. Such is the way out of worrying about the bad seeds in play for Carroll too, if we recall Sylvie's decision to play for company, shrinking and self-effacing as she is, because of the pleasure her music will give *them*.

As summed up by William Madden in "The Victorian Sensibility": "Between 1800 and 1900 intellectual and moral assent had shifted from an order outside and prior to the self to an order, so far as there was order at all, that had to be created from within and was co-extensive with the self."[49] Charlotte Yonge was quite out of date by 1900. As the century progressed, purely internal referents (what she would have called selfish) were being more and more admitted as legitimate motives to action. One obvious example is art for art's sake, which follows an aesthetic very close to Schiller's when he links art with play and separates it from utility and teaching. As Carroll realized, science itself, the great work of the

---

[48] Yonge, *The Heir of Redclyffe* (New York, 1871). See also her "Amusement" in *Womankind* (New York, n.d.), pp. 120–121: "Just as play is necessary to children, so play or pleasure of some kind is wholesome for the average human being"; the young girl is quite safe "whose great aim is to make things pleasant for other people."

[49] Madden, "The Victorian Sensibility," *Victorian Studies*, VII (Sept. 1963), 93.

nineteenth century, might often enough be found on examination to be a form of sport.

Lewis Carroll was aware of the extent to which people might live by, and perhaps run into dangers through, "an order . . . created from within and . . . co-extensive with the self." One name for that order is play. He never calls for the reinstitution of the gospel of work, but he would have liked to introduce an antidote to the destructive egoism that he himself portrays so damagingly (while so fetchingly) in the games of *Alice*, the sport of *Sylvie and Bruno*, and the hunt of the *Snark*. In the preface to *Sylvie and Bruno Concluded* Carroll makes an appeal common enough for an inhabitant of a country and a century whose certainty of an "order outside and prior to the self" had been almost evolutionized and aestheticized away, although it is perhaps not quite the appeal one expects from the uncommon creater of the moral-less if not irreverent play worlds of the *Alices*; he calls for "the revival, in Society, of the waning spirit of reverence" (II, xxiii). Carroll espouses what can be called a gospel of amusement, or play. He shows us at the same time that not all in the gospel is holy.

Index

213

Play, Games, and Sport

Designed by R. E. Rosenbaum.
Composed by York Composition Co., Inc.
in 12 point intertype Weiss, 1 point leaded,
with display lines in Weiss.
Printed letterpress from type by York Composition Co., Inc.
on Warren's No. 66 text, 50 pound basis,
with the Cornell University Press watermark.
Bound by Vail-Ballou Press
in Columbia book cloth
and stamped in All Purpose foil.